Structured Sensory Intervention for Traumatized Children, Adolescents and Parents

STRUCTURED SENSORY INTERVENTION FOR TRAUMATIZED CHILDREN, ADOLESCENTS AND PARENTS
Strategies to Alleviate Trauma

William Steele
and
Melvyn Raider

Mellen Studies in Social Work
Volume 1

The Edwin Mellen Press
Lewiston•Queenston•Lampeter

Library of Congress Cataloging-in-Publication Data

Steele, William.
  Structured sensory intervention for traumatized children, adolescents, and parents : strategies to alleviate trauma / William Steele and Melvyn Raider.
    p. cm. -- (Mellen studies in social work ; v.1)
  Includes bibliographical references and index.
  ISBN 0-7734-7347-5
  1. Post-traumatic stress disorder--Treatment. 2. Psychic traauma--Treatment. I. Raider, Melvyn. II. Title. III. Series.

RC552.P67 S74 2001
616.85'21--dc21

2001042765

This is volume 1 in the continuing series
Mellen Studies in Social Work
Volume 1 ISBN 0-7734-7347-5
MSSW Series ISBN 0-7734-7353-X

A CIP catalog record for this book is available from the British Library.

Copyright © 2001 William Steele and Melvyn Raider

All rights reserved. For information contact

<table>
<tr><td>The Edwin Mellen Press
Box 450
Lewiston, New York
USA 14092-0450</td><td>The Edwin Mellen Press
Box 67
Queenston, Ontario
CANADA L0S 1L0</td></tr>
</table>

The Edwin Mellen Press, Ltd.
Lampeter, Ceredigion, Wales
UNITED KINGDOM SA48 8LT

Printed in the United States of America

DEDICATION

To Shirley Dobie for your dedication, patience, passion and understanding.

William Steele

TABLE OF CONTENTS

INTRODUCTION   1

CHAPTER ONE   5
Trauma Defined

CHAPTER TWO   19
*Evolution of Posttraumatic
Stress Disorder and Interventions*

CHAPTER THREE   29
*Conceptualizations of Trauma Interventions
for Children and Adolescents*

CHAPTER FOUR   37
Field Testing and Research

CHAPTER FIVE   49
*Evaluation Research Study: Structured Sensory
Intervention for Traumatized Children, Adolescents and Parents*

CHAPTER SIX 63
  Overview: Structured Sensory Interventions for Children, Adolescents and Parents (SITCAP)

CHAPTER SEVEN 83
  Beginning the Intervention: Focus and Strategy Sessions

CHAPTER EIGHT 107
  Parent Model

CHAPTER NINE 151
  Debriefing: Trauma-specific Interventions for Schools and Agencies

CHAPTER TEN 187
  Intervention Questions, Answers, and Anecdotal Accounts

BIBLIOGRAPHY 209

INDEX 219

LIST OF ILLUSTRATIONS, FIGURES, TABLES

Table 1: Type of Problem	39
Table 2: Mean PTSD Score by Problem Type	40
Table 3: PTSD Score by Problem Type	41
Child Adolescent Questionnaire Subscale Means	54
ANOVA Group Difference	55
Average Mean Reduction of Reactions	56
ANOVA Group Differences of Average Mean Reduction	56
Demographics of Subjects	57
Psychosocial History of Subjects	57
Three month Follow-Up Mean scores	59
ANOVA Identified Group Differences	59

PREFACE

Traumatic experiences disrupt the lives of countless children, adolescents and adults. Trauma is not specific to violence but can result in the aftermath of natural disasters, chronic and acute illness, illness or death of a parent, accidents, dog bites, separation from a parent, and divorce. Many children and adolescents exposed to potentially traumatic situations fail to receive developmentally appropriate intervention. The situation is complicated in that the symptoms of posttraumatic Stress Disorder (PTSD) can mimic and co-exist with other conditions. However, mis-diagnosing traumatized children and adolescents with primary Oppositional Defiant Disorder and Attention Deficit Hyperactivity Disorder diminishes treatment effectiveness. Clinicians frequently ask for assessment and practical treatment guidelines for children and adolescents who have experienced single and multiple traumas. Mr. Steele and Dr. Raider have provided an essential guide for use in a broad array of settings, including agencies, hospitals and schools.

The <u>Structured Sensory Interventions for Traumatized Children, Adolescents and Parents</u> (SITCAP) model is a comprehensive treatment approach designed to diminish the terror that exposed individuals experience and facilitate feelings of safety. Trauma reactions are normalized and the distinction between trauma and grief is emphasized. This structured protocol provides a valuable session-by-session, situation specific (e.g., school vs. agency) guide to intervention. It is appropriate for individuals who have experienced violent or non-violent trauma and is age-specific (preschoolers, 6-12 year olds, adolescents, adults). Focusing on themes such as 'hurt and 'worry' that accompany both violent and non-assaultive types of trauma enhances the generalizability of the model. The parent component encourages a supportive caretaker response and addresses past and present traumas in the parent's life.

The SITCAP model utilizes a series of drawing tasks and treatment specific questions that focus on the ten major sensations that follow trauma (e.g., terror, fear, worry, powerlessness). The premise is that traumatic memories are experienced at a sensory level and must be reactivated in order to be moderated and tolerated with a renewed sense of power and feeling of safety. The nonverbal act of drawing coupled with the repeated exposure of telling the narrative helps transform these symbolic memories into a conscious form that can then be addressed therapeutically. Traditional psychotherapy often encourages the discussion of feelings that has the undesired effect of overwhelming the child. Through a structured drawing process, children are guided through the reliving of the experience and are assisted in telling their story. The trained facilitator then assists them in developing a new narrative that relegates the traumatic memory to the place and time it occurred instead of permeating every aspect of life. The emphasis is on cognitive reframing, taking traumatized children from the passive to an active role so that they feel greater control over the experience. Children, adolescents and their parents are taught that they are survivors.

The SITCAP model has been field-tested and designed for use in the school setting. Although not all exposed children go on to develop severe reactions, there is ample evidence that early intervention can prevent or diminish long-term sequelae. The debriefing process is outlined in detail so that the trained facilitator can quickly intervene in the school setting to assist not only students but staff and administrators.

Following a concise review of the trauma literature, the authors provide a detailed description of trauma interventions for children and adolescents. Chapters addressing field testing and research discuss the limitations of conducting trauma studies. The SITCAP model is outlined in a sequential manner and the basic drawing technique is explained in detail. Illustrative case studies provide rich material for clinicians and demonstrate the benefits from beginning at the sensory memory level. The section on common therapeutic struggles (e.g., What to do if the child refuses to draw) increases the utility of this text. The model acknowledges the potential for therapist victimization (e.g., their safety along with the victims). Addressing an oversight in much of the existing trauma intervention literature, the authors discuss secondary victimization whereby well-intentioned relatives, friends and even professionals offer hollow comments that compound the wound experienced by the victim. The structured activities help victims identify the ways others have inadvertently wounded them and validates their responses.

<u>Structured Sensory Interventions for Traumatized Children, Adolescents and Parents</u> (SITCAP) fills a void in the child and adolescent trauma treatment literature. It promises to be a frequently utilized book in the libraries of psychiatrists, psychologists, social workers, nurses, school personnel and other mental health professionals who encounter traumatized children and their families. The adaptability of the model is one of its greatest strengths as it can be used in a variety of settings.

Marquita Bedway, Ph.D.
Pediatric Psychologist and Adjunct Assistant Professor, Department of Psychiatric and Behavioral Neurosciences, Wayne State University, Michigan.
Co-Director of the ADHD Life Span Center at Wayne State University.

ACKNOWLEDGEMENTS

There are many very special people who were instrumental in making this work possible. Certainly, we cannot thank enough, the two thousand school counselors, social workers, psychologists, school nurses, agency clinicians, child care workers, pastoral counselors, bereavement counselors, and marriage and family therapists who field tested our intervention programs over the past eleven years. To take time out of their already demanding schedules and case loads, demonstrates the commitment to their professions and the children in their care.

Ms. Roberta Sanders, MSW, Executive Director of New Center Community Mental Health Center in Detroit, Michigan was the co-founder of the Institute. It was her desire to address the immediate needs of a community exposed to violence that provided the Institute with it's first home and positioned it to be ready to assist Kuwait citizens after the Gulf War. Her efforts have not gone unnoticed.

Since 1995, Michael Horwitz, ACSW, Executive Director of the Children's Home of Detroit (CHD), has provided unlimited support for the development, field-testing and research of TLC interventions and it's resource material and "Tools to Help the Helper". Mr. Horwitz and William Rands III, CHD Board Trustee, made it possible for The National Institute for Trauma and Loss in Children (TLC) to expand it's training, services and programs nationally. This national exposure has significantly enhanced the value and accessibility of the Institutes' interventions.

We certainly want to acknowledge TLC's National Advisors. Over the past several years they have provided invaluable clinical recommendations regarding

TLC's intervention strategies. Their varied professional disciplines have greatly assisted the development of intervention programs which address varied needs and situations. Thank you for your expertise: Marquita Bedway, Ph.D., Adjunct Professor, Department of Psychiatry and Behavioral Sciences and Co-Director of the ADHD Lifespan Center, Wayne State University; Noreen Brohl, MSW, School Social Worker, Michigan; Kathryn Brohl, MA, LMFT, Trauma Consultant in private practice, Florida; Deanne Ginns-Gruenberg, BSN, MA, LPC, RPT-S, Registered Play Therapist in private practice, Michigan; David Grill, MA, MFCC, CTS, Clinical Director of the Trauma Treatment Center for Traumatic Life Experiences, California; Cathy Malchiodi, MA, ATR, author and Director of the Institute for Arts and Health in Utah; Marie Nelson, M.Ed.; Patti Porter, M.Ed. and Dee Ingle, M.Ed., Trauma School Specialists and Consultants, Texas; Barbara Oehlberg, MA, Child Development Consultant, Ohio; Mary Pappas, MA, Jungian Therapist, Illinois; and Linda Whitney Peterson, Ph.D., tenured Associate Professor of Pediatrics and Psychiatry, University of Nevada School of Medicine. Again, your international experiences, expertise and guidance has had major impact on the formation of the intervention programs detailed in this book.

We are very thankful for the patience of our typesetters and editors. Their attention to detail and ability to consistently assist with our multiple revisions has been remarkable. Deva Ludwig, Mary McHenry and Philip Ernzen, thank you so much for your attention to detail and pursuit of quality.

Our acknowledgement would be incomplete if we did not mention the thousands of traumatized children and families who, in the midst of their pain, were still able to teach us all the meaning of being a survivor. Their willingness to participate in TLC's efforts in order to afford those that followed with field-tested interventions has been very special. As special, have been the many schools and communities who have allowed TLC and it's Certified Trauma and Loss School Specialists and Consultants to assist them following school related and community shootings, suicides, accidental deaths and other critical incidents. The uniqueness of each situation and all those involved certainly enriched the many intervention strategies, protocols and procedures established by the Institute and incorporated into it's SITCAP model.

FOREWORD

The visibility of children in distress is increasingly brought to the attention of human service professionals by the media and within practice settings as professionals witness, first hand, children being exposed to natural disasters, war, violence, family disruption, and social upheaval. Our idealism about childhood suggests that it is a time when children should be children, that they should enjoy a protected period of innocence and that they should be able to grow and develop under what we understand to be the optimal conditions of human development.

Unfortunately, the intrusion of seriously traumatic events can compromise even the most resilient child. It is a sad commentary on modern times that so many children are exposed to traumatic events. Periods of trauma can persist for some children and can become emotionally overwhelming, changing their feelings and behavior permanently. Witness the many children worldwide who are exposed to war and who witness violence on a too frequent basis. Witness the many children who are exposed to death and murder. Professionals may want to recoil from the images such events can produce in their minds. But trauma is a very real aspect of contemporary human service practice.

This is a book of hope and optimism even though trauma itself can overwhelm those who provide care. For sure, it is a book about the personal and social problem of trauma, but also it is a book that offers human service professionals a clear pathway to address, resolve, and mitigate the serious consequences and toll trauma can take on children and their families. The authors have done the hard work to clear this pathway, to articulate it, and to light it. The authors have made explicit their thinking about trauma in childhood and adolescence, they have reviewed the state of the art, and they have formulated a specific model to guide action. In the work entitled "Structured Sensory Intervention for Traumatized Children, Adolescents, and Parents (SITCAP)," the authors have field tested their approach using an integrated strategy of intervention, and they have examined quite closely the effects of the intervention on children in school, agency, and community settings.

It is one thing to undertake research to document a social problem. However, it is quite another challenge to craft a promising model of practice to address a specific issue, to submit this model to trial use, and to examine how it performs in relationship to the resolution of its initial objective. This is why this book is so important. The authors have moved through these research and development stages with an explicit intent in mind: to reduce the negative mental health and emotional consequences of trauma among children and to facilitate their functioning and well being. The data they incorporate into the book, quantitative, qualitative, and case-oriented, offers evidence that SITCAP can relieve trauma and reduce its impact. The procedures they highlight give relevant and meaningful direction to even the most experienced human service professional.

This book is practical in its design and content. The reader will find key definitions, rationale, theory, and practice that the authors combine in ways to illuminate the dynamics of childhood trauma and to specify strategies of intervention. Practice data and information sit on a strong intellectual base that links to psychiatric concepts and theory and historical analysis of the idea of trauma. Early in the book the authors set the stage for the concept of trauma and illustrate its evolution during the course of the Twentieth century. Later in the book they detail the design and the knowledge base of the model.

It is difficult to witness the exposure of children, their parents and siblings to trauma. But this book reminds us that we should not be pessimistic about what the human service community can do about it. This is a book that empowers, enlightens, and encourages. Read it and grow in your ability to assess trauma. Study it closely and you will learn practical ways to intervene and to change the course of trauma. Read it and become proactive.

David P. Moxley, Ph.D., D.P.A.
Professor of Community Practice and Social Action
School of Social Work, Wayne State University
Detroit, Michigan

INTRODUCTION

Recent school violence, with it's impact on children and adolescents, has highlighted the urgency to identify effective treatments for complicated grief and posttraumatic stress disorders. The rash of school violence has prompted parents, teachers, social workers, counselors, administrators and policy makers to learn more about posttraumatic stress disorder, (PTSD) in children and adolescents. It is now accepted that children can and do experience all the reactions of posttraumatic stress (PTSD) following both violent and non-assaultive incidents. Research since the mid 1980's to date clearly validates the existence of PTSD in children exposed to violence (Pynoos and Nader, 1988; Black, Hendricks and Kaplan, 1992; Dykman, McPhearson and Ackerman, 1997). Violence has been an epidemic among young people since the mid 1980's. The 1999 violent killings at Columbine High School in Colorado only heightened awareness and the seriousness of violence in this country.

However, trauma is not specific to violence. Natural disasters such as fires (McFarlane, Policansky & Irwin, 1987; March, Jackson, Costanzo & Terry, 1993) hurricanes (Lonnigan, Shannon, Finch, Taylor & Daugherty, 1991; Vernberg, Eric, LaGreca, Silverman & Prinstein, 1996), boating disasters (Yule, 1992), burns and other serious accidents, and medical procedures such as bone marrow transplants (Stubner, Nader, Yasuda, Pynoos & Cohen, 1991) can also induce PTSD reactions in children and adolescents. Living with a terminally ill adult or sibling, drownings, house fires, car fatalities, living with substance-abusing parents and divorce were also found to be identified as incidents preceding the onset of PTSD in children (Raider, Steele & Santiago, 1999).

The reactions which can be experienced following a trauma can significantly impact learning, behavior, social, emotional and psychological functions. These reactions can be induced by either violent or non-assaultive incidents of the type previously detailed. Hyperarousal, for example, is a manifestation of trauma that directly alters basic learning functions. Two children with the same I.Q. will function and perform entirely different if one is put into a hyperarousal state following trauma exposure. The hyperarousal child will have difficulty processing verbal information (Perry, 2000). Constantly fearful and hypervigilant children focus on non-verbal cues. It becomes a way of preparing for what is "seen" as a potential threat. Because of the difficulty in processing verbal information using the neocortex, the hypervigilant, traumatized child has difficulty learning. Learning is just one area impacted by trauma exposure.

In more recent years professionals (van der Kolk, 1994; Levine, 1997) have more readily supported the concept that the "body remembers" and that trauma is experienced at a sensory level and stored as an implicit memory. Individuals exposed to trauma experience images, sensations and impulses that are detached or disconnected from a more cognitive understanding of what is happening. To help trauma victims, we now understand that we must help the victim at a sensory level before his experience can be understood at a cognitive level. Implicit memory (sensations of trauma) must be linked with explicit memory (the facts or reality of the incident) in order for the victim to be able to now reorder the experience in a way that in the present is now manageable (Rothschild, 2000). Knowing the ways in which trauma is experienced by its victim gives us critical information to design our intervention.

Structured Sensory Intervention for Traumatized Children, Adolescents and Parents (SITCAP) is an intervention model proven effective and valuable in both school and agency settings. This book will detail the model, its foundation, strategies, field testing and research. The model addresses interventions for children and adolescents three through eighteen years of age, for parents of traumatized children, and for parents who themselves have been traumatized. The case examples and description of session activities address the unique parameters of intervention in school environments, as well as the more clinically focused interventions in agency settings.

When a trauma-inducing incident exposes a school population, several additional levels of intervention are necessary (Johnson, 1993; Petersen and Straub, 1994; Williams et al. 1994). Crisis intervention, organized protocol, and classroom presentations are critical the first three days. From the third day through the following six to eight weeks, varied levels of debriefing are necessary for the most exposed students/clients and staff at different times for different purposes. Following the Acute Stress period (4-6 weeks following exposure), more trauma-specific intervention will be needed for those who fulfill criteria for posttraumatic stress disorder (PTSD). Surviving parents and parents of the most exposed often themselves become vulnerable to trauma symptoms as well. The SITCAP model also addresses the unique intervention needs of these parents, schools, staff and students.

Although research is limited in its study of intervention outcome for traumatized children, adolescents and parents; research is abundant in its identification and description of trauma and its discussion of the needs of traumatized victims. A brief review of the history, and research related to trauma and PTSD is essential for understanding the needs of victims and direction of intervention.

The first five chapters will lay the foundation for the core intervention strategies of the programs making up the SITCAP model. Field-testing and research results of these strategies will also be reviewed. The remaining chapters will detail the intervention process and answer a number of process questions related to when to use which type of intervention. A number of case examples will be presented that focus on specific SITCAP activities directed at helping victims find, at a sensory level, relief from the terror of their experiences.

CHAPTER ONE
Trauma Defined

Trauma has had many names. Cardiac neurosis, soldiers' irritable heart, shell shock, gross stress reaction and transient situational disturbance were some of the terms used to define what is now called posttraumatic stress disorder (PTSD).

The concept of trauma actually dates back to 1860 when the British reprinted descriptions of victims' reactions following severe train wrecks. The accounts identified both physical and emotional distress in those victims. Ericksen (1860) attributed these conditions to hysteria, a condition Ericksen and his contemporaries claimed only occurred in women (van der Kolk, 1996). Many argued that the symptoms of "railroad spine" had resulted from extreme fright, and therefore these reactions were psychological in nature (van der Kolk, 1996). The attempt to attribute emotional distress reactions to the psychic reaction Freud (Piers 1996) called hysteria did not have wide acceptance, as most believed only woman experienced hysteria. Freud (Piers, 1996) believed that an incident became traumatic as a result of the person's psychological state of mind, which does not allow it to rid itself of the experience. The struggle between organic and psychological origins of trauma persisted for over one hundred years. In the field of thaumatology today, there is far greater support for posttraumatic stress having psychological as well as neurological origins.

Reports of children's reactions to extreme stress, such as war, appeared in significant numbers during and following World War II. During this period of time the American Psychiatric Association also acknowledged that normal persons exposed to intolerable stress were vulnerable to trauma. Unfortunately children were largely neglected in the pursuit of understanding trauma until the 1980's, when a good deal of research was initiated to formally study the impact of violence on children.

Today the literature is abundant with studies detailing trauma-specific reactions found in children following exposure to both violent incidents and those incidents in which perpetrated assault was not involved. Fires, accidents, critical injuries, divorce, separation from parent, respiratory arrests, cancer, surgery and catastrophic events such as floods and hurricanes have all been shown to induce posttraumatic stress disorder in children. The criteria for PTSD is based upon the criteria found in the Diagnostic and Statistical Manual of Mental Disorders (DSM-IV) (APA, 1994) but, also documented criteria that have been established since the publishing of the DSM-IV.

Prior to the 1994 DSM-IV publication, children had not been included in the PTSD diagnostic category. Children in fact were not part of the field study group used to establish the DSM-IV definition and criteria for PTSD, even though children were included under PTSD for the first time in 1994 by the American Psychiatric Association. Since 1994 a great deal of research has documented numerous trauma reactions in children. Accordingly children are now part of the field study group being evaluated for future revisions of criteria and symptomatology.

Posttraumatic Stress Disorder

Posttraumatic stress disorder is defined in the Diagnostic and Statistical Manual of Mental Disorders (DSM-IV) published by the American Psychiatric Association (1994).

For posttraumatic stress disorder to exist in either children or adults, two characteristics must exist:

1) The person experienced, witnessed, was related to, or was confronted with an event or events that involved actual or threatened death or serious injury or threat to the physical integrity of self or others.

2) The person(s) response involved intense fear, helplessness or horror... in children (it) may be expressed instead by disorganized or agitated behavior.

The PTSD diagnosis can be made when the following criteria also exists.

1) The traumatic event is persistently re-experienced in one (or more) of the following ways:
   - Recurrent and intrusive distressing recollections of the event, including images, thoughts or perceptions. In young children, repetitive play may occur in which themes or aspects of the trauma are expressed.
   - Recurrent distressing dreams of the event. In young children, there may be frightening dreams without recognizable content.
   - Acting or feeling as if the traumatic event were recurring (includes a sense of reliving the experience, illusions, hallucinations and dissociate flashback episodes, including those that occur on awakening or when intoxicated). In young children, trauma-specific reenactment may occur.
   - Intense psychological distress at exposure to internal or external cues that symbolize or resemble an aspect of the traumatic event.
   - Physiological reactivity on exposure to internal or external cues that symbolize or resemble an aspect of the traumatic event.

2) Persistent avoidance of stimuli associated with the trauma and numbing of general responsiveness (not present before the trauma), as indicated by three (or more) of the following:
   - Efforts to avoid thoughts, feelings, or conversations associated with the trauma
   - Efforts to avoid activities, places, or people that arouse recollections of the trauma
   - Inability to recall an important aspect of the trauma
   - Markedly diminished interest or participation in significant activities
   - Feeling of detachment or estrangement from others
   - Restricted range of affect (e.g. unable to have loving feeling)
   - Sense of a foreshortened future (e.g. does not expect to have a career, marriage, children, or a normal life span)

3) Persistent symptoms of increased arousal (not present before the trauma), as indicated by two (or more) of the following:

- Difficulty falling or staying asleep
- Irritability or outbursts of anger
- Difficulty concentrating
- Hypervigilance
- Exaggerated startle responses

Additional Criteria

Pioneers in childhood trauma like Robert Pynoos, Ph.D. and Lenore Terr, MD have established more detailed descriptions of the ways trauma manifests itself in children. Pynoos and Nader (1988) classified child symptomatology into pre-school, third through fifth grade and adolescent reactions. These reactions include:

Pre-school Symptomatology
"Generalized fear, cognitive confusion, lack of verbalization, attributing magical qualities to traumatic reminders, sleep disturbances, anxious attachment, regressive symptoms, anxieties."

Third through Fifth Grade Symptomatology
"Preoccupation with their own actions during the event, specific fears, retelling and replaying of the event, impaired concentration and learning, sleep disturbances, concerns about their own and others safety, inconsistent behavior, somatic complaints, feeling confused, disturbed and frightened by their grief responses, fear of ghosts, concerns for other victims and their families and close monitoring of parent responses and recovery."

Adolescent's Symptomatology
"Detachment, shame, guilt, self consciousness about their fears, vulnerability and other emotional responses, acting out behavior, life threatening reenactment, abrupt shifts in relationships, desires to take revenge, radical changes in life attitudes, premature entrance into adulthood."

This breakdown provides for a more descriptive view of PTSD, but presents limitations as criteria for actual assessment of PTSD. On the other hand, these classifications and descriptions provide directives for suggested interventions.

Udwin (1993) summarized the findings of Terr (1981, 1985) Pynoos and Nader (1988) and Yule (1991). Sleep disturbances, loss of newly acquired skills, concentration difficulties, memory impairment, persistent intrusive thoughts and images, raised levels of anxiety – generalized and specific, heightened alertness (hypervigilance) and survivor guilt were all identified as reactions specific to posttraumatic stress.

Johnson (1993) also classified reactions by school age. Unlike Pynoos, however, Johnson separated reactions within each age level into four categories: cognitive, physical, emotional and behavioral. On the preschool category, for example, he lists some of the following:
- Cognitive – shorter attention span, confusion regarding event, location, sequencing, death.
- Physical – loss of appetite, overeating, bowel/bladder problems, sleeping disturbance.
- Emotional – generalized fears, nervousness, anxiety, irritability, fearful of reminders.
- Behavioral – bed wetting, thumb sucking, nightmares, repetitive play, anxious attachment, clinging, aggression, disobedience.

Peterson and Straub (1992) identified additional reactions not described by others: increased aggressive conduct, dullness, decreased trust in adults' ability to protect, sensitivity to feelings of shame and being stigmatized, premature and unforgiving of their own behavior.

The literature abundantly documents that children and adolescents can experience posttraumatic stress disorder following violence and other critical incidents of real or perceived threat to the physical integrity of the individual or others. Acknowledging the vulnerability of traumatized children and adolescents to posttraumatic stress disorder has encouraged researchers to examine intervention outcomes.

Recognition of Trauma Reactions in Normal Adults and in Children

One importance of World War II was the defining of PTSD, and detailing the symptoms of children and adolescents. Bradner (1943) made direct reference to children's posttraumatic fears, nightmares, arousal and other symptoms. In addition, survivors of concentration camps were studied, especially those survivors of Nazi Germany concentration camps, which revealed the inadequacies of psychiatric terms to describe these experiences and effects (Frankl, 1960).

The other major change resulting from World War II experience was that large numbers of persons with normal personalities, broke if the stress was too high. The psychiatrists with exposure to "front line" trauma in soldiers recognized that to date the "psychiatric community had failed to recognize the significance of the trauma itself (Kinzie, Goetz, 1996 p.167)." This initiated a rethinking of the need for premorbid conditions to exist to diagnose trauma.

The wealth of the data emerging from the War was so compelling that the American Psychiatric Association included in the DSM-I (APA, 1952) the classification of gross stress reaction. The acknowledgement that the diagnosis applied to previously more or less, normal persons who experienced intolerable stress was also significant.

Diagnosis of Posttraumatic Stress Disorder

Following the Korean War and throughout the 1950's and 1960's a good deal of research continued on veterans and new research emerged on civilians who experienced natural and industrial disasters (Quarentelli, 1985). Bloch, Silber and Perry (1956) reported on the impact of a Mississippi tornado that devastated an entire town. These and other incidents (e.g., the sinking of the Andrea Doria and the 1962 Alaskan earthquake) served to identify the unique reactions of trauma survivors.

The DSM-II published in 1968, omitted the gross stress reaction Classification and replaced it with transient situational disturbance which included acute reactions to overwhelming environmental stress (APA, 1968). However, there were no operational criteria for formulating this diagnosis.

In the early 1970's rape trauma syndrome was established and led to additional research. Ann Burgess and Linda Holstrom at Boston City Hospital first described the rape trauma syndrome (van der Kolk, 1996). They indicated that symptoms were similar to those of surviving veterans. Research on family violence began about the same time and included battered children.

In time, a consensus began to arise from these studies that any normal person could develop symptoms if the stress was intense enough. The DSM-III (APA,1980) initiated the posttraumatic stress disorder category still in use today. It indicated that the stressor "producing this syndrome (PTSD) would evoke significant symptoms of distress in most people and is generally outside the range of such common experiences as simple bereavement, chronic illness, business losses or marital conflict." Theory and practice were brought together as a result of this criteria. The DSM-III R (revised edition) added to the earlier criteria age-related features of PTSD but still provided little information relative to the expression of symptoms in youth.

The DSM-IV further enhanced the criteria for PTSD and added a new disorder, Acute Stress Disorder (APA, 1994). It specified types of traumatic experiences and indicated that PTSD could be induced by observing such events or being the recipient of information about the stressful events of others. It also stated that "sexually traumatic events may include developmentally inappropriate sexual experiences without threatened or actual violence (APA, 1994)." It further indicated that PTSD symptoms may be preceded by acute stress, that PTSD symptoms may emerge within the first three months following the trauma, or that there may in fact be a delay of several months or years before onset of symptoms.

There are others today (Herman, 1992, van der Kolk, 1996, Saigh and Bremmer, 1999) who have indicated a need to go beyond the DSM-IV PTSD category to address those who have endured prolonged traumatic stressors and conditions. There was an attempt to include in the DSM-IV "disorders of extreme stress not otherwise specified" (DESNOS). However, it was not included. The World Health Organization's (WHO) (1992), classifications does include reactions for those who have been victimized over prolonged periods. As research continues, so too do changes in the diagnostic classification and categories related to traumatic exposure.

Causes and Identification of Trauma Reactions in Children

Research examining trauma reactions in children and adolescents is now extensive. Violence in this country precipitated a good deal of research as to the impact of violence on children and revealed strong evidence that "acute posttraumatic stress symptoms result from violent life threat, and that severity is related to the extent of exposure to the threat or witnessing of injury or death (Pynoos, Nader, Arroyo, et al., 1987)."

Famularo, Kinscherff and Fenton (1992) described trauma reactions induced by physical and sexual abuse. Trickett and Putnam, (1993), and Deblinger, Lippman and Steer, (1996), delineated trauma reactions induced by being a witness to parental homicide and other forms of violence. Pynoos, (1987); Terr (1990) and Saigh (1991) described trauma reactions created from the exposure of living in violent communities. Garbarino (1992) and Wallen (1993) also detailed trauma reactions seen in children from violent environments.

However, it was later determined that trauma was not specific to violence. Natural disasters such as fires (McFarlane, Policansky & Irwin,1987; March, Jackson, Costanzo & Terry, 1993), hurricanes (Lonigan, Shannon, Taylor, Finch & Salee, 1991; Vernberg, Eric, LaGreca, Silverman & Prinstein, 1996), boating disasters (Yule, 1992), burns and other serious accidents, and medical procedures such as bone marrow transplants (Stubner, Nader, Yasuda, Pynoos & Cohen, 1991) were seen to also induce PTSD reactions in children and adolescents. Living with a terminally ill adult or sibling, drownings, house fires, car fatalities, living with substance abusing parents and divorce were also found to be identified as incidents preceding the onset of PTSD in children (Raider, Steele & Santiago, 1999).

Although a good deal of research continues to look at factors of vulnerability and resiliency as predictors of PTSD levels of severity, its duration and chronicity, it is agreed that the diagnosis of PTSD can, in fact, be assigned to children and adolescents.

Additional Considerations

Meichenbaum, (1994) pointed out that posttraumatic stress disorder is the only diagnosis in the entire DSM-IV manual that places the origin of symptoms on external events rather than on the individual personality. Matsakis (1992) stated that regardless of previous factors negatively impacting personality, PTSD does not develop as a result of these factors but because of exposure to a traumatic event. van der Kolk, McFarlane and Weisaeth, (1996), also supported this notion. The APA (1994) identifies a trauma as an incident which is unexpected and is an unusual life event which involves actual or perceived threat to life or ends in death or critical injury. It involves intense fear, helplessness, terror and disorganized or agitated behavior in children.

The DSM-IV was by no means conclusive or comprehensive in its description of PTSD. Survivor guilt, for example, a well recognized, clinically supported reaction to trauma, was not listed in the DSM-IV. Others have argued that categories need to be expanded. Terr (1991) identified two types of trauma. Type I trauma includes single, sudden, isolated events of limited duration. Type II refers to chronic, multiple, long standing, repeated events often of intentional human design, such as sexual assault or combat. van der Kolk, Roth, Pelcovitcz and Mandel, (1993) suggested that the current diagnostic categories failed to address what he and others (Herman, 1992) considered to be additional features of PTSD syndrome.

The literature abundantly documents that children and adolescents can experience posttraumatic stress disorder following violence and other critical incidents of real or perceived threat to the physical integrity of the individual or others. Acknowledging the vulnerability of children to posttraumatic stress disorder has only been recent (APA,1994). Research related to intervention with traumatized children, therefore is limited at this time.

Victim Exposure

Ongoing studies are conflicting when reporting on the relationship of exposure to severity. Exposure refers to the physical proximity to the incident. Pynoos, Nader, Arroyo, et al. (1987) in detailing research following a sniper attack in a California school found that "the children in the area the shooting took place had a higher prevalence of PTSD (94.3 percent) than youth in the school building (88.9 percent), at home (44.2 percent) or on vacation (45.1 percent). Pynoos utilized the PTSD Reaction Index developed by Frederick (1985) and further revised by

Frederick and Pynoos. The Reaction Index incorporated items related to all the symptoms listed in the DSM-III. It has recently been revised to meet the DSM-IV standards.

Related to physical proximity is direct victimization versus non-direct victimization. Schwarzwald, Weisenberg and Waysman (1994) reported that, following Scud missile attacks on Israel, youth who lived in the areas hit had a higher level of PTSD (62.9 percent) than youth living in communities that escaped attacks (24.9 percent). He also found that children whose homes were hit by the missiles had a higher prevalence (23.8 percent) of PTSD than those whose homes had not been hit (9.1 percent). Reports following the 1989 San Francisco earthquake also indicated similar outcome of exposure. Those who lived within one mile of a collapsed freeway were more likely to experience PTSD (50 percent) than those who lived further away (8 percent) (Bradburn, 1991).

However, there are conflicting studies that find proximity not to be related to prevalence of PTSD. Following the 1993 New York World Trade Center bombing, Koplewicz et al. (1994) found that exposure did not relate to PTSD presence, but that youth who experienced both high and low level exposure had comparable prevalence of 66 and 69 percent. Shaw (1995) found similar results after Hurricane Andrew. There were no significant differences between youth who resided in areas that had high and low exposure to the hurricane.

Establishing prevalence of PTSD by exposure appears to have contradictory results. The literature review points out that war events, catastrophic events such as hurricanes and floods, criminal victimization and serious accidents had higher levels of prevalence than did less deliberate events (Saigh, 1999). This in part can be attributed to the variety of tools used to evaluate for PTSD and to criteria used to define "close" and "not close" proximity, such as children trapped in the elevator of the World Trade Center when the bomb exploded versus those on the first floor with easy access out of the building.

The Milgram, Toubiano and Klingman(1988) study of 268 seventh graders following a tragic school bus accident suggested that personal involvement with the victims, rather than the situation itself, could increase level of prevalence. Saigh (1991) also found that non-witnesses who hear of the details of an incident can, in fact, experience PTSD.

The study of children exposed to a variety of incidents has helped to further our understanding of the relationship of exposure to presence and level of severity of reactions. Unfortunately to date, few studies have been identified that examine exposure related to outcome. Examining outcome relationship may help advance our understanding of the relationship of exposure variables to prognosis.

Incident Type

Absent in the literature are studies that examine the type of incident and related prevalence and what similarities or differences across incidents are related to severity levels at the beginning of intervention and following intervention. McFarlane (1987) reported high levels of prevalence 8 and 21 months following a massive fire. Similar levels were reported in children following a school shooting (Pynoos, Nader, Arroyo, et al. 1987).

History documents that women more likely experience personal trauma involving rape, sexual molestation and childhood parental neglect. Except for physical attacks, males are more likely to experience impersonal traumas such as fires, floods, disasters, combat and witnessing the injury of others (Saigh, 1999). Sexual trauma is reported to have the highest incidence of PTSD in males and females. It is possible, therefore, that the variables of personal versus impersonal nature of an incident are predictive or related to intervention outcome.

Worry

van der kolk (1996) identified worry about the safety of a family member or friend following an incident as one of six factors involved in the complexity of a child's reaction to trauma. Schwarz and Kowskie (1991) also reported that worry about the safety of self and others was related to proximity of sixty-four children interviewed following a school shooting in an elementary school in suburban Chicago in 1988. The female adult perpetrator killed one child and wounded six other children before leaving the school and killing herself at a nearby home. Questions about worry for the safety of loved ones, about the family of the deceased child and injured children and worry about personal safety were asked.

Eighty one percent of the children worried about someone during or following the event. The author suggests that worry as an "emotional state" may be equivalent to proximity to the event and a variable in symptom formation. Longigan et al. (1991) also found that children with high levels of worry were more likely to experience PTSD.

Worry appears to be related to presence of severity of reactions and a general response to trauma. If worry is an indicator of severity and PTSD presence, several questions that need to be examined emerge: Is the severity of the worry identified by the victim related to the levels of severity of trauma reactions? Is the focus of that worry related to severity levels of reactions? If worry is a variable of trauma and can be measured as to its severity following trauma, will a positive or negative change in the severity level of worry relate to reductions or increases in severity of trauma reactions following intervention?

The Nature of the Incident

Herman's (1992) study of extreme trauma involving multiple incidents or a prolonged incident shows that such trauma attacks the personality. She writes (p.86) "While the victim of a single acute trauma may feel after the incident that she is not herself, the victim of chronic trauma may feel herself to be changed irrevocably or she may lose the sense that she has any self at all." If that is the case, we would expect that outcome gains would be much less than with those who experienced a singular event. Terr (1991) supported Herman and indicated that Type I traumas (single unanticipated events) do not "appear to breed the massive denial, psychic numbing or personality problems that characterize the Type II (chronic/multiple) traumas." It is conceivable, however, that some individuals may be predisposed to Type II reactions following a singular Type I event because of personal history that has induced strong levels of vulnerability and "psychic fragility" that cannot withstand, or adequately recover from, a Type I experience.

It is important to evaluate the relationship of these dependent variables to severity and outcome to support earlier findings but also to identify possible differences with earlier findings. van der Kolk (1996), Mechenbaum (1994) and others indicate that not all persons exposed to Type I and Type II traumas will in fact experience PTSD. It is possible therefore that some of the participants exposed to multiple or chronic trauma are able to realize significant reduction of their trauma reactions. And, if this is the case, there will be similarities or differences that explain intervention outcomes experienced within Type II participants.

There remains a need for comprehensive research to answer the questions raised in this discussion on the relationship of variables to severity. While this research continues, exploration and research is also needed to understand those factors that contribute to successful intervention outcomes. The research examining intervention outcomes with traumatized adults is far more abundant than research of intervention strategies with traumatized children and adolescents. The information available about adult intervention has, however, created a foundation from which to develop and explore similar intervention strategies with children and adolescents.

CHAPTER TWO
Evolution of Posttraumatic Stress Disorder and Interventions

The Civil War and every war the United States has been involved in since the Civil War continued to refine the work on trauma initiated by the British in 1860. The question of whether trauma resulted from organic causes versus psychological causes directed and dictated the focus of intervention. A brief examination of the history of trauma from the Civil War, World War I, World War II, and post World War II provides an understanding of the foundation of intervention being provided today.

Civil War - World War I

The struggle between mind-body origins persisted for another one hundred years after the Civil War. The Civil War and World Wars I and II were instrumental in making a distinction between organic and emotional sources of trauma. During the Civil War soldiers exposed to combat were examined for increased arousal, irritability and elevated heart rate. These symptoms were called "DaCosta's Syndrome" or "Soldiers' Irritable Heart" and were determined to be due to "a physiological disturbance related to exposure to the stress of combat" (Saigh, Bremmer, 1999). Attributing posttraumatic problems to the heart continued through World War I. It was referred to as "cardiac neurosis," "disorderly action of the heart" or "neurocirculatory asthenia" (van der Kolk, 1996). Historically, contributing PTSD symptoms to organic causes has provided an honorable solution to the traumatic reactions of soldiers in combat. It prevented humiliation in soldiers, a "rational" cause for psychological breakdown which could not be explained at the time, and preserved soldier morale and the war effort itself.

Myers (van der Kolk, 1996) was the first to use the term "shell shock" but discovered that similar reactions could be found in those not exposed to war. He later played an important role in rejecting trauma reactions as being a source of organic causes and emphasized the close relationship between hysteria and war neurosis.

Freud attributed trauma to a psychic reaction rather than to the result of an external event. Hysterical symptoms he wrote (Piers, 1996, p. 540), "have revealed causes which must be described as psychic traumas. Any experience which arouses the distressing affects...can have this effect and it obviously depends on the sensitivities of the person concerned whether the experience acquires the importance of a trauma."

Earlier Pierre Janet described trauma as a dissociative response, a view that was later supported and pursued by William James, Jean Piaget, Henry Murray and Carl Jung. Janet suggested that when people experience overwhelming emotions their minds might not be able to match these frightening emotions within a cognitive framework. As a result "the memories of the experience can not be integrated into personal awareness. Instead, they are split off (dissociated) from consciousness and from voluntary control" (van der Kolk, 1996, p. 52). Accepting the dissociative model led to disagreement with Freud's notion that catharsis and abreaction were the treatment of choice. Janet's followers supported synthesis and integration of the experience (into personal consciousness).

Between World War I and II

Psychoanalytic influences had little impact on prevention and early intervention in clinical settings following World War I and did not result in institutional change (van der Kolk, 1996). The one major change that did develop was initiated by Abram Kardiner who worked with traumatized U.S. War veterans and completed analysis with Freud. Following these experiences Kardiner reassessed his observations but was unable to successfully create a theory of war neurosis based upon the earlier psychoanalytic theory. Despite this failure, his meticulous and detailed description of symptoms helped more than anyone else had to define PTSD for the remainder of the 20th Century (van der Kolk, 1996; Kinzie and Goetz, 1996).

Kardiner wrote that "'pathological traumatic syndrome' consists of an altered conception of the self in relation to the world, based on being fixated on the trauma and having an atypical dream life, with chronic irritability, startle reactions, and explosive aggressive reactions" (van der Kolk, 1996, p. 57). Kardiner believed that the traumatized individual's response to trauma was to protect against its recollection. This effort to avoid recollection, he believed, left individuals stuck in their trauma, which eventually led to a futility that "often overtook them; they became withdrawn and detached, even when they had functioned well prior to combat" (van der Kolk 1996, p. 57).

Between the World Wars the initiation of the study of non-war-related trauma was begun. Traumatic neurosis and physical trauma were studied following injuries in the industrial environment. The focus on "industrial trauma" was complicated by compensation issues and legal opinions. The outcome of this focus was that "the physician delineates signs and symptoms; the legal system decides on compensation" (Kinzie and Goetz, 1996 p.166).

World War II

At the start of World War II there had been little change in the way trauma was conceptualized or treated because the lessons of the previous war had been forgotten. In the United States an effort was made by U.S. psychiatrists to apply Kardiner's work to combat treatment. "Front line" psychiatry was initiated in order to provide a more immediate response as well as recovery (Belenky, 1987). This effort set the stage for research as well as applied intervention with adults. Kardiner's observations about the persistence of profound, conditioned, biological responses were confirmed, and somatic interventions introduced. Hypnosis and narcosynthesis were used to help victims remember and abreact the trauma. Janet's earlier findings were also supported, and the U.S. pioneered the use of a group stress debriefing (Shalev and Ursano, 1990). Group therapy emerged during this period as well.

Post World War II

New information about the psychophysiology of trauma is now receiving very close attention and is directing intervention that is "sensory oriented" as well as medication orientated. Today, posttraumatic stress disorder is treated with varied intervention approaches: psychotherapy, debriefing, Eye Movement Desensitization Reprocessing, Stress Inoculation and Thought Reduction Therapy, and medication. Despite differences which exist between modern trauma therapists and the followers of Freud, Janet, Kardiner and others, there are critical areas of agreement that direct the major intervention strategies of today (Piers,1996).

There is agreement that behavior can be influenced by "non-conscious mental content" and that repressed trauma memories can alter behavior and personality. There is agreement that the mind can hold on to stressful experiences through adulthood and that trauma can remain active in its influence on behavior and personality. There is also consensus that any normal person can develop posttraumatic stress disorder if the stressor is intense enough. Most importantly there is agreement that the trauma experience needs to be integrated into consciousness and the person's experience of self, so the individual is no longer controlled and "directed" by the experience.

Contemporary Intervention With Adults

Foa and Kozak (1985) stated that two conditions were required for the treatment of PTSD and the reduction of fear:

1) The traumatic memories must be reactivated in order to be modified. The ability to decrease fear or anxiety is dependent upon the controlled reliving

of that fear in a safe environment so as to be able to diminish the response to it; and,

2) Corrective information must be provided so that the victim can form a new narrative or meaning that places the traumatic memory to the place and time it occurred as opposed to generalizing that experience to everyday life.

Exposure techniques were designed to help the trauma victim realize that their trauma memories and reactions are not dangerous and do not need to be avoided. Exposure refers to revisiting the details of the experience. Exposure strategies help the victim learn to tolerate the once intense fear and emotional reactions of their traumatic experience. Once this is accomplished, the victim can reorder this experience at a cognitive level into a meaningful narrative that is now manageable. Exposure methods do vary in the way they are conducted.

Systematic desensitization is the repetitious return to details of the incident until the anxiety associated with the recall is distinguished. It uses brief, imaginal and arousing experiences. "It pairs imaginal exposure with relaxation so that the anxiety elicited by the confrontation with feared stimuli is inhibited by relaxation" (Saigh, 1999). Wolpe pioneered this approach which was used to treat combat and rape victims.

Imaginal exposure has the client relive the traumatic experience by recounting it in detail aloud. Clients are instructed to visualize the experience as they describe it; to talk about it as if it were happening now. As much detail as possible is given. This results in the forming of a traumatic narrative that is repeated until the client no longer has reactions to the memories.

"In vivo" exposure consists of actually placing the client in situations similar to the trauma. These are safe situations not dangerous replications. The client is physically exposed to each component of the experience until the fear response is distinguished or becomes manageable. Not every feared aspect or trigger needs to be dealt with in this fashion due to the generalization that takes place during this exposure process.

Cooper and Clum (1989) studied imaginal exposure as an additional intervention to outpatient treatment and found that it enhanced improvement in combat veterans. Keane, Fairbank, Corddell and Zimering (1989) found similar results in their study, in addition to the reduction of reexperiencing symptoms of PTSD. Prolonged exposure, usually "imaginal" and "in vivo" exposure, was studied for outcome results on female assault victims by Foa, Dancu, Hembrel, et al (1997). The exposure group was compared to those groups receiving stress inoculation training, supportive counseling, and a wait list group. In follow up studies of up to one year, exposure technique results were superior in outcome to the comparative groups. Thompson, Charlton, Kerry et al. (1995) and others have shown significant results in the reduction of trauma when using exposure techniques with a variety of traumatic experiences.

Trauma specialists today frequently combine exposure therapy with cognitive therapy. Cognitive therapy believes that trauma victims' emotional reactions are driven by their thoughts. Two victims exposed to the same situation may therefore react differently based upon the way each interpreted (thought about) the situation. The more disturbing trauma reactions are driven by more dysfunctional thoughts. Cognitive therapists believe that changing the thoughts changes the emotional reactions.

Cognitive therapy helps the client first identify the thoughts (traumatic memories), evaluate their validity, challenge erroneous or defeating and destructive thoughts and then replace these with thoughts supportive of health or manageable emotional states (Saigh, 1999). This process is referred to as cognitive restructuring.

The studies on the effectiveness of cognitive therapy with PTSD are fewer, but those that do exist strongly suggest its value and efficacy. Cognitive therapy becomes beneficial in the integration of trauma memories into conscious memories. In other words the thoughts associated with the trauma experience are altered to reflect current life space. They are reordered in a way that memories now become manageable. An example might be, "I survived this experience; I will survive other experiences because it has prepared me, made me stronger, etc." This is sometimes referred to as survivor thinking versus victim thinking.

Frank (1988) found that cognitive therapy was beneficial in alleviating post-assault and chronic post-rape reactions with women. Although cognitive restructuring studies are limited, their outcome certainly supports their efficacy with PTSD, especially as an adjunct to exposure therapy. Cognitive therapy has become a component of Stress Inoculation Training (Meichenbaum, 1974), one of the anxiety management treatments for PTSD which studies support as an effective treatment of PTSD. Cognitive therapy is used to provide a rationale for why victims should expose (relive) themselves to the pain of their experience. It is also used to reframe their perception of that experience and as a means of stopping dysfunctional thinking. Overall the use of exposure and cognitive-based therapies have shown to be effective and essential components of successful PTSD therapy with adults.

The Psycho-Physiology of Trauma

Trauma is a sensory experience (Lang, 1979) that can initiate a heightened physiological arousal state in response to sounds, images, sensations of touch, smell, and in rare cases taste. Thoughts (memories) of the trauma can also trigger or sustain the arousal response (van der Kolk, 1996).

"Understanding the physiology of trauma is understanding the normal life-preserving survival responses of fight/flight/freeze in an individual and how they fulfill nature's species-preserving function. Investigating the disturbance of those responses forms the essential foundation for understanding pathology that results in posttraumatic stress and posttraumatic stress disorder" (Grill, 1999).

A traumatic stress reaction is manifested physiologically by activation of the autonomic nervous system, increased muscular tension, the release of certain hormones into the blood and reduced or intensified responses of the immune system (van der Kolk, 1996).

The initial reaction to acute threat or stress is survival reflex-alarm and readiness. This triggers a response designed to resist or solve the threat, which often includes the response of fight, flight, or freeze. If resolution is successful, arousal is decreased to its pre-trauma level. If the response to the trauma is never completely discharged, there remains a "readiness" and an "alert" state of arousal. In the heightened continual arousal state the person is constantly on alert even without a trigger (stimulus associated with trauma). This leads to being frozen in this state in which the individual cannot modulate the arousal response nor appropriately discriminate levels of threat.

A more detailed description of the psychophysiological, neurohormonal, and psychobiological impact of trauma is outside the scope of this section. However, it is important to understand that, while in an increased arousal state, serious short term memory suffers (Starknum, Gebarskie, Berent, & Schteingart, 1992) in ways similar to that of Cushing's disease. Verbal memory also decreases (Bremmer et al, 1995). Physiological arousal also triggers trauma-related memories, and these memories then precipitate generalized arousal (van der Kolk, 1996). High levels of arousal also produce changes in neuronal excitability, often manifested in aggression or exaggerated withdrawal (safety response), (Le Doux, Romanski, & Xagoraris, 1991). In essence both memory and emotions are altered by trauma (Saigh, 1999) which in turn leads to problems with learning, relationships, and performance.

Learning can be altered due to the change trauma initiates in processing verbal and non-verbal information. In the hyperarousal state the traumatized victim is unable to use the neocortex to process verbal information. It becomes difficult to process and store verbal information. The traumatized child's learning will be largely in the sub-cortical and limbic areas that deal with non-verbal information. (Perry, 2000). Hand gestures, facial expression, full body posturing all become far more important to survival than verbal information while in the arousal state. These functions, therefore, make it difficult for the traumatized child who's arousal level remains high, to effectively learn. Often these children are labeled as Learning Disabled or having Attention Deficit Hyperactivity Disorder. Interventions, therefore, needs to address the reduction of hyperarousal.

The post-traumatic stress experience is a sensory one that terrifies and creates anxiety. This is also referred to as "implicit" or "procedural" memory. "Declarative" or "explicit" memory refers to the conscious awareness of facts or events. Implicit memory refers to how an event is remembered by the body and central nervous system (van der Kolk, 1996, Squire, 1994, Rothschild, 2000). The trauma experience is stored implicitly via images, sensations, affective, and behavioral states.

Understanding the sensory nature of trauma has led to varied treatments to deactivate the autonomic hyperarousal state by using the body (sensory elements) as a resource to resolve its symptoms. Eye Movement Desensitization and Reprocessing (EMDR), Thought Field Therapy (TFT), Traumatic Incident Reduction (TIR), and Visual Kinesthetic Dissociation (VKD) are being used to reduce or eliminate the arousal state so the survival reflex can complete its response and allow the victim to experience a "sensory relief" followed by healing.

The SITCAP model developed by TLC uses a series of drawing tasks and trauma-specific questions that focus on the major sensations that follow trauma: fear, terror, worry, hurt, anger, revenge, accountability, absence of a sense of safety, powerlessness and victim versus survivor perceptions of self and the world. Any one of these sensations can become a major theme (pattern) that drives the trauma victim's thinking and behavior. SITCAP devotes entire sessions to each sensation/theme to insure the child, adolescent or parent is given the opportunity to expose the intervenor to those sensations/themes that are most severe.

These adult intervention strategies are being used as the framework for intervention with traumatized children. These strategies are reviewed in greater detail in Chapter Three to better understand the application with children and adolescents. Several key intervention concepts described in this chapter will also be repeated in Chapter Three because of their importance in directing intervention applied to children and adolescents.

CHAPTER THREE
Conceptualizations of Trauma Interventions for Children and Adolescents

The majority of conceptual models cited to support trauma-specific interventions relate to use with the adult population. The question as to their application to children and adolescents six through eighteen years of age is critical and needs further research. The following conceptualization and research support the interventions of SITCAP, it's history, research and practice.

McFarlane (1988) stated that intrusive reliving rather than the traumatic incident itself was the cause for the complex biobehavioral change referred to as PTSD. Repeated intrusive thoughts and images "fix" the individual into a state of attempting to avoid this reexperiencing of the trauma. Traumatized individuals have difficulty with such intense and overwhelming reactions and become unable to utilize emotions as guides for actions. van der Kolk (1996) indicated that PTSD caused people to "experience their internal world as a danger zone that is filled with trauma-related thoughts and feelings. They seem to spend their energy on non thinking and planning. This avoidance of emotional triggers further diminishes the importance of current reality and paradoxically increases their attachment to the past." Intervention needs to be directed at safely reliving the trauma in order to operate in the present and be reconnected to the future.

Piers (1996) described this constant (fixed) memory of the trauma experience as being "triggered by similar auditory, visual, affective and relational cues." Freud believed that the ego would actively attempt to rid itself of a traumatic experience "by an effort of will." Freud also believed that trauma was not the result of an incident itself, but was "an interaction between the patient's intrapsychic organizing tendencies and the external event." (Piers, 1996). The trauma therefore was seen as a psychic one, not an external one. Freud basically suggested that an incident became traumatic as a result of "psychology of unique sensitivities of the patient." Both views considered trauma to be experienced at a sensory level.

Trauma theorists (Piers, 1996) suggested, on the other hand, that trauma was "split off (dissociated) from the rest of the mind and remains there through a concrete, structured partitioning of the mind." Trauma theorists suggested that the trauma incident would be remembered in an unmodified form, not in symbolic representation as suggested by Freud. Since trauma is defined symbolically, intervention must allow for the symbolic communication of what that experience was like.

Despite the differences that exists between modern trauma theorists and Freud, there are critical areas of agreement. Piers (1996) writes,

"They agree that human actions can be influenced by non conscious mental content (repressed trauma memories can alter behavior and personality)...that the mind can preserve impressions from childhood long into adulthood (trauma remains active in its influence on behaviors, personality)...and that (most critically) the trauma experience needs to be integrated into consciousness (or the) patient's larger experience of self."

Motivated by the theoretical belief that trauma needed to be integrated into consciousness, Freud and other analysts worked at bringing the trauma experience into consciousness and helping the patient provide a detailed account of the experience (Piers, 1996, Emery, 1996).

Exposure Based Treatment

Re-exposing the trauma victim to his experience became and has remained a core component of adult trauma intervention. It is now a primary strategy with children. Deblinger, Lippman and Steer, (1996) in working with sexually abused children used exposure techniques to significantly reduce overall PTSD symptomatology. Malleson (1959) defined a form of exposure described as "in vitro" exposure used to reduce severe anxiety. Stampfl (1961) combined Mallesons' exposure techniques with that of Freud's approaches to develop "implosive therapy." This was a process of identifying cues triggering the trauma memories and reactions, and then exposing the client to these cues repeatedly until extinction of the trauma reactions resulted.

Rachman (1966), Marks (1972), Mellen and Levine (1984), Saigh (1987), and others have utilized exposure as a core process in helping trauma victims integrate their experience into consciousness. van der Kolk (1996) stated,

"Traumatic memories need to become like memories of every day experience, that is, they need to be modified and transformed by being placed in their proper content and restructured into a meaningful narrative."

Psychodynamic and cognitive-behavioral treatment agree with this desired outcome even though different approaches may be utilized.

Exposure Techniques

Exposure techniques are derived from learning theory. Mower's (1960) two factor theory was at the core of the variety of exposure techniques that have been developed. Mower suggested that fear was "acquired via classical conditioning, when a neutral stimulus is paired with an aversive stimulus or unconditioned stimulus. The neutral stimulus now a conditioned stimulus comes to illicit a fear response" (Saigh, 1999). Fear is maintained through operant conditioning (reexperiencing of aspects of event) and the efforts to avoid or escape these responses.

In trauma, even when the unconditioned stimulus is removed (the incident itself), the continued attempts to avoid the fear prevents the realization that the conditional stimulus no longer leads to negative consequences. In other words, the avoidance efforts support the fear. When traumatic memories are not integrated into consciousness via activating exposure to them and then modifying them into an integrated memory, the memories then continue to trigger the traumatic state or conditioned responses.

Exposure techniques are designed to help the trauma victim realize that the conditioned responses are no longer dangerous and avoidance no longer necessary. The ability to learn to tolerate the intense fear and emotional reactions experienced by a traumatic event is a critical part of recovery. From here the experience can be modified or reordered, into a form that is acceptable and manageable by the victim - a cognitive restructuring (corrective information) into a meaningful, integrative narrative.

As detailed in the previous chapter, Foa and Kozah (1985) stated that two conditions were required for the treatment of PTSD and the reduction of fear:
1) The traumatic memories must be reactivated in order to be modified. The ability to decrease fear or anxiety is dependent upon the controlled reliving of that fear in a safe environment so as to be able to diminish the response to it; and,
2) Corrective information must be provided so that the victim can form a new narrative or meaning that places the traumatic memory to the place and time it occurred as opposed to generalizing that experience to everyday life.

Exposure treatment provides the opportunity to relive the trauma to diminish it at a sensory level. Following this the client can then begin the development of the trauma narrative or giving the experience a "language" which can then be reordered at a cognitive level that can now be managed by the client.

Cognitive Treatment

Aaron Beck (1972, 1976) pioneered cognitive therapy which was then further developed by others. The basic component of cognitive theory is that thought drives emotion. Similar situations in individuals may lead to different emotional states based upon the way that situation is interpreted (thought about) by the different individuals. Disturbing, anxiety-ridden, pathological emotional states are driven by dysfunctional thoughts. Cognitive therapy suggests that by changing the thoughts the emotional states change.

Cognitive therapy helps the client first identify the thoughts (traumatic memories), evaluate their validity, challenge erroneous or defeating and destructive thoughts, and then replace these with thoughts supportive of health or manageable emotional states (Saigh, 1999). This process is referred to as cognitive restructuring.

The studies on the effectiveness of cognitive therapy with PTSD are fewer but those that do exist strongly suggest its value and efficacy. Cognitive therapy becomes beneficial in the integration of trauma memories into conscious memories. In other words the thoughts associated with that experience are altered to reflect the current life space. They are reordered in a way that these memories now become manageable. An example of this effort might be, "I survived this experience. I will survive other experiences because it has prepared me, made me stronger." This is referred to as survivor thinking versus victim thinking.

Frank, Andersen and Stewart (1988) found that cognitive therapy was beneficial in alleviating post-assault and chronic, post-rape reactions in women. Although cognitive restructuring studies are limited, their outcome certainly supports their efficacy with PTSD and especially as an adjunct to exposure therapy. Cognitive therapy has become a component of Stress Inoculation Training (Meichenbaum, 1974), one of the anxiety management treatments for PTSD that studies support as effective treatment of PTSD. Cognitive therapy is used to provide a rationale for why the victims should expose (relive) themselves to the pain of their experience. It is also used to reframe their perception of that experience and as a means of stopping dysfunctional thinking.

Overall the use of exposure and cognitive-based therapies are considered to be effective and essential components of successful PTSD therapy.

Drawing

A form of exposure therapy used to assist in constructing the trauma narrative while at the same time reliving that memory is the use of drawing. Cognitive psychology has demonstrated "that memories determine the interpretation of the present even when they are not conscious" (Mihaescu and Baettig, 1996 p. 243). Children experience trauma at a sensorimotor level then shift to a "perceptual (iconic) representation to a symbolic level" (Mihaescu and Baettig, 1996). Later in adult life these memories are ordered linguistically. When a terrifying incident such as trauma is experienced and does not fit into a contextual memory, a new memory or dissociation is established (van der Kolk, 1987). When that memory cannot be linked linguistically in a contextual framework it remains at a symbolic level for which there are no words to describe it. In order to retrieve that memory so it can be "encoded" and given a language and then integrated into consciousness, it must be retrieved and externalized in its symbolic perceptual (iconic) form. Drawing helps to accomplish this externalization. In 1918 on the battle front of La Fauche, France, "drawing was successfully employed to provide access to repressed memories of traumatic scenes" (Pynoos and Eth, 1986 p. 316). Drawing provides a link between dissociated memories and retrieval into consciousness, after which the experience can be translated into narrative form, and then reordered by the child's effort to integrate the experience into his life experiences.

Pynoos (1986) relied heavily on drawing as the primary intervention with children traumatized by violence. The authors indicated (1986) that drawing "invariably signifies the child's unconscious preoccupation with the traumatic memory." Drawing provides for an externalization of the experience and through the motor (drawing) and verbal (giving the narrative) actions, helps move the child from a passive (internal) powerless involvement with the trauma, to an active (external) control of that experience.

Malchiodi (1998) stated that drawing provided children an impetus to tell their story. It provides the child the ability to translate his traumatic experience into a narrative. Riley (1997) indicated that this act (drawing) was a form of externalization, a visible projection of ones self, thoughts, and feelings.

Beyers (1996) described the use of drawing with children and families with PTSD as a result of military conflict in the West Bank and Gaza. She cited numerous studies of the use of nonverbal media (drawing) to assist PTSD children with access to trauma memories, the integration of the "split-off parts" induced by the trauma, and the successful reintegration of these into the child's current understanding of their world. Magwaza, Killian, Petersen, Pillay (1993) formed similar results with South African children exposed to violence. Saigh (1999), in discussing exposure by "flooding," indicated that children might not be able to imagine trauma scenes or tolerate prolonged "in vivo" experiences. Instead he suggested that an "effective adjunct to the more orthodox form of flooding (is) asking traumatized children to prepare sketches of their stressful experience and verbally repeat (narrate) the content of their work (p. 370)."

Drawing provides a method for accessing traumatic memories and bringing them to consciousness. A number of therapists have anecdotally reported on its value for working with victims of violence, such as rape, war, terrorism, as well as with natural disasters (Abbenante, 1982; Golub, 1985; Herl, 1992; Roje, 1995; Webb, 1991). Johnson (1987) suggested drawing (art) as a treatment of choice when working with victims of violence. He, as do others cited, stated that this modality could have a unique role in the early stages of treatment in accessing traumatic memories. Individuals who have experienced trauma may encode such images via a photographic process, and visual modalities may offer a way to bring such images to consciousness. Most suggested that bringing (externalizing) these memories out in this fashion would allow the child to develop a healthy distancing from the self and the painful memories. Once this occurs the need to engage in avoidance is reduced, and relief from trauma induced anxiety decreased.

The National Institute for Trauma and Loss in Children (TLC) began developing and evaluating it's intervention programs in 1990. To date, exposure, trauma narrative and cognitive reframing are the primary interventions. Drawing is used as the primary activity to approach trauma at the sensory level and to assist in the reexperiencing and development of the trauma narrative, which is followed by reordering (cognitively reframing) the experience in a way that is manageable. Chapters Four and Five detail TLC's research and development of it's *Structured Sensory Intervention for Traumatized Children, Adolescents and Parents*. Chapters Six through Ten provide a detailed review of the programs and interventions.

CHAPTER FOUR
Field Testing and Research

Phase I: Initial Exploratory Research and Field Testing

The National Institute for Trauma and Loss in Children (TLC) initiated its first explanatory research in 1990. The study identified a number of questions for future research, some of which have since been answered by other researchers. It provided the documentation needed to support the assertion that children and adolescents exposed to varied violent and non-assaultive incidents could and did experience a range of trauma-specific reactions of mild to severe levels of intensity. It also assisted school counselors, social workers, and agency clinicians with the need to respond differently to the unique needs of the traumatized students and children in their care.

The research project was referred to as the Seven County Trauma Referral Network. Professionals in schools and agencies from seven diverse counties in Michigan participated and later became referral resources for trauma intervention. Using the one session consultation model based upon a model developed by Pynoos and Eth (1986), intervention was provided to one hundred and seventy-nine children, 6-18 years old, who were exposed to either violent or non-assaultive incidents that induced trauma-specific reactions. The Pynoos PTSD Child Reaction Index was used to assess PTSD symptoms. This is a 20 item scale used in a semi-structured interview. This tool identified the presence of post-traumatic stress reactions and their levels of severity. The main purpose of this intervention effort was to evaluate the children, parents, and therapist's responses to this one session format and the identification of trauma-specific reactions triggered by varied incidents.

The one session format utilized drawing and a series of trauma-specific drawing tasks and questions to guide the child through the process of exposure and trauma narrative. TLC developed specific trauma questions to facilitate the development of forming the trauma narrative and to focus on major themes and sensations associated with traumatic experiences.

Methodology

- A total of 150 professionals were trained by the TLC Institute to use the project's posttraumatic stress disorder (PTSD) assessment and intervention tools and strategies.
- Fifty-eight (58) agencies from seven diverse counties in Michigan were represented by these participants.
- A total of 179 PTSD assessments/interviews were completed. Children were assessed utilizing the Pynoos PTSD Child Reactions Index and provided a single session intervention based on the Pynoos model.
- The children ranged from three (3) years of age to seventeen (17) years of age; 94 of the children were 10 years of age or younger.
- The situations children were exposed to included the following:
    a. murder of sibling or parent;
    b. witness to murder, rape, physical abuse, domestic violence;
    c. abandonment by parent;
    d. separation from parent due to substance abuse, physical/sexual abuse or neglect;
    e. chronic addiction of parent;
    f. natural death of parent, grandparent;
    g. death by house fire, car accident, drowning;
    h. suicide death and/or attempted suicide of parent or sibling;
    i. shooting of friend;
    j. homelessness;
    k. chronically mentally ill parent

l. frequent hospitalization of parent;
m. divorce;
n. discovery of body.
- Development of a Parent Guide was completed and provided to parents of children and adolescents assessed. It identified the differences between grief and trauma and ways to help their children.

Quantitative Data Analysis

Types of problems or nature of the traumatic incident were coded into 10 categories (Table 1). The categories were as follows: parent murder/suicide, other murder/suicide (other family member or significant other), parent death, other death (terminal illness, car accident, house fire, drowning), abuse/neglect (self or sibling), substance abuse (family member), sexual abuse (self or sibling), domestic violence (self or family member), witness to violence (outside the home), and other (kidnapping by father, father denied paternity, violence to friend not witnessed, divorce, critical injury due to dog attacks, accidents). Every effort was made to fit the incident into the best category to capture the nature and intensity of the incident/occurrence.

Table 1
Type of Problem

Problem	N	%
Parent Murder/Suicide	12	6.7
Other Murder/Suicide	9	5.0
Parent Death	10	5.6
Other Death	10	5.6
Abuse	42	23.5
Substance Abuse	13	7.3
Sexual Abuse	18	10.1
Domestic Violence	13	7.3
Witnessed Violence	7	3.9
Other	45	25.1
Total	170	100

Of the 179 cases for which data was collected and the Pynoos and Nayder PTSD Reaction Index administered, 166 inventories were completed without error. Thirteen inventories had at least one missing data point in the reaction index. These 13 cases had to be excluded from the analysis since a valid PTSD raw score could not be calculated.

Additionally, nine cases were missing the year of the occurrence, two cases were missing the present age of the child, and eight cases were missing the child's age at the time of the occurrence as well as the time since the occurrence. Table 2 reflects the Mean PTSD score by problem type for the 166 valid cases.

Table 2
Mean PTSD Score by Problem Type

Problem	Mean PTSD
Parent Murder/Suicide	44.00
Other Murder/Suicide	30.71
Parent Death	43.77
*Other Death	39.11
Abuse	37.78
Substance Abuse	41.36
Sexual Abuse	43.00
**Other	35.86
Domestic Violence	39.84
Witnessed Violence	36.00
Total Mean	38.64

* = Other Death – terminal illness, car accident, house fire, drowning.
** = Other – kidnapping by father, violence to friend not witnesses, divorce, separation, critical injury.

An analysis was conducted on the data to explore the relationship of the independent variables of age at time of trauma, elapsed time since incident, and type of problem/incident. In this analysis the raw score for PTSD was used rather than the severity categories, (i.e. mild, severe, very severe, etc.) since the raw scores captured more information than the categories. Using the raw score a test of mean differences for different values of the independent variables was conducted.

The first independent variable tested was the Type of Problem. All problems, violent and non-violent, showed PTSD presence. Overall, the type of problem did not have an impact on the magnitude of the PTSD score (Table 3). Traumas such as the murder or suicide of a parent resulted in the highest average PTSD raw score, but this was only slightly higher than the PTSD score for children who lost a parent to another cause of death other than violence.

This appeared to indicate that any type of parental death was very traumatic for children. Sexual abuse and substance abuse in the household were also related to high levels of PTSD.

Table 3
PTSD Score by Problem Type

Problem	Mean PTSD
Parent Murder/Suicide	44.00
Other Murder/Suicide	31.00
Parent Death	43.00
*Other Death	39.00
Sexual Abuse	42.00
Other Abuse/Neglect	38.00
Substance Abuse Parent	41.00
Domestic Violence	36.00
Other Witnessed Violence	37.00

The categorical nature of the independent variable precluded the use of the Analysis of Variance, but a Chi-Square test performed on the categorized PTSD reactions revealed no statistical relationship overall. A One Way Analysis of Variance test was also conducted and found no statistically significant differences between the groups based on the type of problem. This suggested that the differences in the means of the PTSD Raw scores among trauma types were not large enough to be significantly different statistically, given the small numbers of cases in each group.

This result may have been the function of using categories that were too broad for problem types. It is suggested that it may be necessary in the future to identify more specific circumstances of the trauma itself. Witnessing the murder of a parent, for example, may produce more intense trauma than learning that a parent has been murdered as now suggested in the literature. It is also suggested that future research use a scale that would rate the circumstances of the trauma on an ordinal scale. Such a scale would enable more discrimination in the intensity of the trauma to the child.

Analysis of the elapsed time since the trauma and the age of the child at trauma showed no significant differences and did not reveal any obvious systematic pattern in the distribution of the scores. The distribution of the means for these variables appeared to be random.

Single Session Introduction

The session began with a brief education about trauma that was directed at normalizing any of the reactions participants may have experienced. They were then asked to draw a picture of what happened. Intervenors were provided a list of questions to ask the participants that were designed to obtain the details of their experience; who was there, what was said, what they were doing at the time or immediately following the trauma, what they thought the people involved were thinking, what was said by those involved, what was said to them (the participants) afterwards, and how others responded to them following their experience.

Participants were then asked to draw a picture of the person who was killed, died, was attacked, injured, at the time of the victimization. Some participants were actual surviving victims, others were eyewitnesses, and others were neither victims nor witnesses but related to the victim. Those who were surviving victims drew pictures of the way they looked at the time of traumatization. A list of additional trauma-specific questions was provided to the intervenor. These questions were directed at specific reactions participants may have experienced then, or continued to experience. Issues of anger, revenge, accountability, hurt, and fear were of primary concern.

Intervenors were given some latitude at this point to explore any of the reactions identified and to ask participants to draw additional pictures related to details of the story as needed. However, careful instructions were provided to leave ample time to conclude the interview. Intervenors summarized what the participant presented, gave the participant an opportunity to review and to add any details to their drawings or story if needed, normalized reactions identified in the process, and prepared participants for future reactions they may yet experience, as a way of defusing anxiety that might otherwise accompany future reactions.

All intervenors began the process with the understanding that additional intervention may be needed and that either themselves or others would need to be immediately available. As this was an exploratory project, maintaining the emotional safety of participants was a primary concern.

Conclusions

- Children as young as three (3) years of age could and did experience PTSD, a diagnosis once only attributed to adults.
- PTSD was not specific to victims of violence or those who witnessed a murder. Children who experienced losses from, or were witnesses to or related to the victims of, car accidents, home fires, terminal illness, and even divorce also rated severe for the presence of PTSD reaction.
- Since PTSD was not specific to violence, many questions could be asked as to what elements in these non-violent situations may have contributed to trauma responses, what previous experiences might have intensified reactions, and was the intensity greater with some symptoms than with others?
- This multi-sensory intervention could actually trigger previous traumatic memories for some children.
- There appeared to be no difference between the severity levels for those who just recently experienced a traumatic event and those who were evaluated years after the event. There were, in fact, indicators that the longer a child went without intervention, the greater the severity of the symptoms.
- Children and adolescents took to drawing easily, especially the drawing of the victim.

- The structure of the interview process, the tasks and the questions provided the intervenors with a sense of safety from their traditional more open-ended approach to intervention.

Recommendations

Based upon the findings described in this study, we recommended:
- Development of ongoing sessions or activities that would be trauma-focused and would be provided over a short period of time, six to eight weeks. This would provide the child a greater opportunity to face all aspects of his/her trauma as often as needed in order to bring relief and, most importantly, a renewed sense of control over his/her life.
- Development of written and visual materials to guide counselors through this process, as the resources which existed at the time were limited.
- Development of resource materials for parents and the children.
- Development of an index assessment that would be age appropriate for children under eight (8) years of age.
- Development of a group intervention process that, via group activities, could identify the possible presence of trauma in addition to grief, and, through group activities to be used in schools and agency settings, could bring relief to those who have been assessed to be experiencing trauma; and
- Continuation of research that would examine the elements of different loss situations to change the focus from viewing a particular event as trauma or non trauma to viewing elements of any loss that have a relationship to PTSD, such as proximity, substance abuse, single parent family, multiple losses, what is seen, heard, etc.;
- Development of a structured debriefing process for helpers to help them manage the stress that can not be avoided when they are being repeatedly exposed to traumatized children.

Following this study numerous research articles began to appear that documented the inducement of trauma from natural disasters such as fires (March, Jackson, Costanzo, & Terry, 1993), hurricanes (Lonigan, Shannen, Taylor, Finch, & Salee, 1991), and other non assaultive incidents. Numerous studies emerged showing that physical proximity (witnessing) was correlated with increased frequency (severity) of reactions (Eth & Pynoos, 1994). These and other studies were detailed in the previous chapters.

Phase II: Development and Evaluation of an Eight Session Intervention

In 1993 the Institute developed and initiated field testing of its *I Feel Better Now!* program, a trauma intervention group program for children six through twelve years old. This is an eight session intervention that focuses on the major themes of fear, terror, worry, hurt, anger, revenge, accountability, safety, power, and survivor thinking versus victim thinking. Worry, safety, power, survivor versus victim thinking were undeveloped themes in the initial exploratory research. The program was field tested in thirteen school districts and three community agency settings. The agency settings included a community mental health center, a YWCA, and a not-for-profit counseling agency serving primarily foster care children.

The program was two years in development. The successful outcome of the 1990 exploratory research led to the development of sessions for each specific theme and drawing activities with trauma-specific questions directed at details of the incident and reactions to the trauma. Added to this effort, which was not available during the initial exploratory research, was the structuring of statements to assist in the cognitive reframing of the way children might, as survivors, now view their trauma experience.

The Institute had been exposed to a number of survivors and survivor groups between 1990 and 1993. This exposure allowed the Institute to integrate into the *I Feel Better Now!* program, specific activities to encourage and support movement from victim to survivor thinking. The Michigan Chapter of Parents of Murdered Children, the Detroit-formed group Save Our Sons and Daughters, and countless child and adolescent survivors helped to identify the type of thinking that allowed those exposed to tragic traumas in their lives survive that tragedy rather than remain in the tragic victim state. The cognitive reframing components added to *I Feel Better Now!* were of great assistance not only for the children but also for the intervenors who themselves needed to learn what it meant to be a survivor and ways that survivor thinking would be integrated into the intervention process.

The use of drawings, exposure, trauma narrative, and cognitive reframing were very structured and specific to each theme. The sessions were designed as two hour sessions. A maximum of eight children exposed to either violent or non-assaultive traumas were assigned to groups. An exception was made for physically and sexually abused children who were placed in sexual/physical victims groups only. One hundred and fifty children completed all sessions of the program. Participants were selected based upon the intervenor's knowledge of the participant's exposure to trauma and reaction manifestations following exposure.

An abbreviated intake form asked parents questions about their children's behavior before and after the trauma. Questions reflected PTSD criteria. Parent satisfaction surveys were completed along with interviewer accounts of participant's behavioral changes observed throughout the eight sessions and their stated comments about changes in emotional status throughout the program. An assessment tool was not used in this field testing other than self report measures by the parent and the child following the program.

Formal research was unfortunately not an option. The major forms of documentation along with the intervenor's summary reports were the parent satisfaction surveys and self report measures of the children, the children's worksheets depicting worry before and after intervention and drawings depicting the way they were feeling before and after.

The intervention process was tightly structured. Intervenors followed structured directions and activities for each session. Worksheets for these activities were provided to the children. Worksheets had specific directions in "title" form; *This Is My Biggest Worry* and *This Is How My Big Worry Is Now*. Interventions are reviewed in detail in Chapter seven.

It was recommended that groups be made up of children six to eight years, eight to ten years, and ten to twelve years of age. The groups were closed. Once initiated, no new members were admitted. The primary ground rules were that only one person talked at a time and that at no time was anyone allowed to draw on or take another child's drawings. The intervenors were instructed that any child who was unable to follow these rules needed to be removed and seen individually. Confidentiality was also a rule.

All drawings were to be kept by the intervenor until the final session, at which time the children's workbooks were returned to them. The seventh session of this program involved the parents. The purpose of this session was to provide each child the opportunity to tell his story to his parent (make the parent a witness). This session was considered critical to healing, as it was designed to help the parent understand, first hand, how the trauma impacted her child, so she could also more readily support the recommendations intervenors provided to help their child heal. Commitment of parent involvement was obtained at the initial session with the parent.

Field Testing Outcome

Parent observations of their children's behavior, mood, and interaction with others following intervention were compared to the same information obtained at the initial parent session. Copies of children's drawings were made. Intervenors also gathered together for a one-day feedback session following the completion of the program.

The Parent Satisfaction form asked the parents if they would recommend the program for others and what positive or negative changes they observed in their children following their participation. One hundred percent of the one hundred sixty parents who responded recommended the program be available to the others and saw moderate to major changes in their child's overall behavior, moods, and interactions. Twenty percent reported that, although there were some positive changes, there were also some areas that saw no change. This is consistent with the formal research findings detailed in the next chapter, which will review the formal research of the Institute's individual intervention program.

All field testers reported a number of outcomes that supported the value of this program for traumatized children. All fifteen groups of children indicated that they did not want their group to end. Field testers reported that they observed significant changes in their children and that teachers and parents also volunteered similar observations throughout the program duration. All reported that the children were eager to draw and to tell of the details of their experiences. The drawings that depicted how each child felt at the time of the trauma and how they felt at the end of the group program all depicted feeling better. Statements like "I'm happy now", "I feel better now", and "I'm okay now" reflected the majority of the responses.

An interesting outcome of the program applied to those groups of children exposed to violent (excluding physical/sexual abuse) and non-assaultive trauma. Ultimately the type of trauma did not matter. The children focused on their reactions not the incident. Fear and worry, for example, were sensory experiences following exposure that they could all relate to, despite having different experiences. This supported the Institute's subsequent decision with the individual intervention program to focus on the sensations of trauma not the child's adaptive behavior. What children reported liking most about being in the group was talking about feelings, telling stories, drawing, and "doing things that made us feel better."

Although funding prohibited formal evaluations, the interviews with children, the feedback from the field testers, the anecdotal stories and accounts, and the parent self-satisfaction surveys all made a strong case for the value of the program. Seven years later the *I Feel Better Now!* Program continues to be used in schools and agencies across the country. The need to conduct formal research to validate the long-term effects of the Institute became of paramount interest following the success of this program.

In 1997, following additional experiences with violent and non-assaultive trauma in schools and communities, including Kuwait following the Gulf War, the Institute developed an individual program for children and adolescents that was field tested and underwent formal evaluation.

CHAPTER FIVE
Evaluation Research Study
Structured Sensory Intervention for Children, Adolescents and Parents

Trauma Intervention Model: Children and Adolescents

The *Trauma Response Kit* now referred to as the *Trauma Intervention Program for Children and Adolescents* was field tested and evaluated in 1997-1998. It is the individual intervention component of SITCAP for children six through twelve years and adolescents thirteen through eighteen years. It was developed in response to the positive outcomes of the Seven County Referral Network and *I Feel Better Now!* exploratory research and field-testing. The model is similar to these earlier efforts in its focus on the major sensations and themes of trauma and its use of exposure, trauma narrative and cognitive reframing. Its major differences accommodate the different developmental levels, individual versus group processes, and a more extensive focus on the use of drawing to address the major sensations of trauma.

Independent Variable

An eight-session trauma-specific, individual intervention protocol for children 6-12 years of age and a second protocol for adolescents up to 18 years of age was developed with the assistance of six trauma experts. Seven of the eight sessions were individual. One of the eight involved both the child/adolescent and parents.

There was an additional individual intake session for parents. Exposure via drawing, trauma narrative, cognitive reframing and education were the major interventions used in this structured model.

Each 50 minute session was designed for use in either school or agency settings. All sessions were formatted with session objectives followed by structured activities designed to achieve the session objectives. Step by step instructions were provided for each activity along with scripted reflections to present to participants, as well as notes to clinicians addressing possible cautions or suggestions related to responding to the participant. Each session used drawing as the primary change process with a focus on trauma-specific sensations/themes, such as terror, hurt, anger, revenge, accountability, and safety.

Activity worksheets corresponded with session activities and were included in a workbook format. One workbook was designed for children and the other for adolescents. Intervention combined drawing related to trauma-specific themes, accompanied by trauma-specific questions related to those sensations used to encourage the participant to tell his story in detail. This was followed by reflections designed to normalize or reframe those trauma-specific reactions presented and their associated sensations.

The intervention process utilized the following techniques:
1) Normalization through education;
2) Understanding through cognitive restructuring;
3) Anxiety management through psychomotor activities;
4) Empowerment through discovery and reframing of responses; and
5) Relief through telling and showing, (exposure to trauma reminder), restructuring and replacement.

The goals of this trauma-specific intervention mode were:
1) Stabilization (return to previous level of functioning or prevention of further dysfunction);
2) Assessment of the child's coping skills;
3) Identification of PTSD reactions;
4) The opportunity to revisit the trauma in the supportive, reassuring presence of an adult (professional) who would understand the value of providing this opportunity;
5) An opportunity to find relief from their terror;

6) An opportunity to re-establish a positive "connectiveness" to an adult;
7) Normalization of current and future reactions;
8) Support of the child's heroic efforts to become a survivor rather than a victim of their experience;
9) Replacement of the child's traumatic sensory experience with positive experiences;
10) Identification of additional needs and recognition of the role parents could take to help meet these needs.

Dependent Variables

Based on posttraumatic stress symptoms specified in the DSM-IV (APA 1994), symptoms were operationalized with the use of two instruments developed by the researchers for this evaluation. The Child and Adolescent Questionnaire (CAQ), a self-report instrument, was a modification of the Child PTSD Reaction Index used by Frederick, Pynoos, and Nader (1992). In the CAQ ambiguous and double-barreled questions were eliminated, and language and vocabulary appropriate for children 6 to 12 years of age, as well as adolescents, were substituted.

The CAQ consists of 35 Likert-type questions comprising three sub-scales. Subscale I is the re-experiencing of the traumatic event, Subscale II is avoidance of stimuli associated with the traumatic event, and Subscale III is symptoms of increased arousal due to the traumatic event. The Parent Questionnaire (PQ) was developed to capture parent-observed perceptions of their child's symptomatic behaviors. It consists of 22 Likert-type questions with no subscales.

Reliability and Validity of Dependent Variable Measures

Both the CAQ and the PQ were judged to have content validity by a panel of six trauma clinicians. The panel reviewed each item for its age appropriateness, clarity, and relationship to DSM-IV PTSD diagnostic criteria. The panel also offered suggestions as to the wording of specific questions in the CAQ to be appropriate to the cognitive level of the subjects. Following revisions, a second review was completed. One hundred percent agreement by all clinicians of the appropriateness of each item was mandatory before inclusion of each item.

Internal reliability was assessed at intake, termination and three-month follow-up utilizing Cronbach's alpha. Reliability of the re-experiencing traumatic event subscale of the CAQ was r=.82 at intake, r=.86 upon completion of intervention and r=.87 at three month follow-up. Reliability of the avoidance subscale of the CAQ was r=.78 at intake, r=.80 upon completion of the intervention, and r=.82 at three month follow-up. Reliability of the arousal subscale of the CAQ was r=.73 at intake, r=.75 upon completion of the intervention, and r=.76 at three month follow-up. The reliability of the Parent Questionnaire was r=.89 at intake, r=.90 upon completion of the intervention, and r=.89 at three month follow-up.

Finally, items from the CAQ, which corresponded to the PTSD subscale from Briere's Trauma Symptom Checklist, were assessed in terms of their reliability as a measure of PTSD. Reliability results were .80 or above for each time period suggesting that the CAQ scale items were comparable to the Briere subscale.

Methodology

Ethical concerns regarding the provision to provide help to children and adolescents who were experiencing painful symptoms of PTSD, as soon as possible, made the use of a random selection, assignment and control group unacceptable. Even though a control group would have enhanced the strength of the findings, the time series design utilized in this study was more suggestive of causality than a simple pre-test/post-test design. Findings were additionally supported by a time series evaluation of parents.

Clinicians who participated in the field-testing of the short-term intervention model were social workers, psychologists, school counselors, mental health counselors, bereavement specialists, childcare specialists, art therapists, and pastoral counselors. Clinicians were recruited from social agencies, mental health clinics and schools to participate in the field testing of the model. They were offered free materials, the *Trauma Intervention Program*, training, and a $100 stipend to participate in the field trial. In exchange, clinicians agreed to utilize the short-term intervention model with five children or adolescents, to administer the CAQ and PQ, and to administer a demographic and social history information sheet to parents of participating children.

Forty-one (41) clinicians participated in the field trial. Ten (10) had a minimum of 16 hours of training, which covered the differences between grief and trauma, DSM-IV criteria, the use of drawing as a process of intervention, and trauma-specific questions to encourage the telling of the story. The remaining 31 clinicians had completed an additional 48 hours of training as part of a certification program for Trauma and Loss Consultant or Trauma and Loss School Specialist provided by The National Institute for Trauma and Loss in Children. All clinicians in the field trial attended a one-day training session on the use of the *Trauma Response Kit*. The purpose of this session was to familiarize clinicians with protocols and forms rather than intervention, as all had a minimum of the same two days of training related to the basic intervention process, as described above. Research requirements, assessment tools, issues related to session activities, and timetables were also covered.

Clinicians obtained parental consent for all participation in the field trial. In addition, consent forms were completed by adolescent participants. The identities of both children and their parents were known only to the clinicians. Researchers received completed instruments that were assigned a case ID number only. Participants were told of all risks and benefits of participating in the trial and were informed that they could discontinue their participation at any time without penalty or continue intervention with another professional if desired.

Clinicians recruited participants into the field trial who had been exposed to one or more traumatic incidents. These included murder, suicide, physical or sexual assault, car fatalities, house fires, drowning, cancer, dog attacks, critical injuries, divorce, foster care placement, or residence with substance abusing parent, or chronically mentally ill parent. Exposure to such incidents included being a victim, being a witness to such incidents, or being related to the victim/survivor. At the time of the first session (intake), exposure could have been as recent as one week prior to intake or up to seventeen years from the date of initial exposure. Questionnaires were administered orally to children and adolescents, while parents were asked to complete their questionnaires in writing. Instruments were administered at intake prior to the intervention model, at termination of treatment (after eight sessions), and three months after the termination of treatment. Parents were seen at intake to complete intake information, which included the Parent Questionnaire (PQ) in addition to a standard family/child psychosocial history. At intake, parents completed the two parts of the Parent

Questionnaire. One was to capture parental recollections of their child's behavior prior to trauma, and the other to record their observations of their child's current behavior. The specific details of the trauma(s) experienced were also obtained at this time. Parents were presented with a video and/or booklet describing the differences between grief and trauma, trauma-specific behaviors, and helpful ways for them to respond to those behaviors. They were informed as to the nature of interventions to be used with their child and the importance of their attendance at two additional sessions. The second session was structured to update them on their child's status, but most specifically to prepare them for their involvement in a parent/child session in which their child would review their story (trauma narrative) developed over the previous six sessions.

Results & Discussion

Analysis was carried out on the entire group of children and parents involved in the study. Since this group included children for whom parents did not complete a parents questionnaire (PQ), a second analysis was carried out on only those children for whom a PQ was completed.

ANALYSIS I
Child and Adolescent Questionnaire

As mentioned earlier, the CAQ questionnaire is composed of three subscales. Subscale I is re-experiencing of traumatic event, Subscale II is avoidance of stimuli associated with traumatic events and Subscale III is symptoms of increased arousal due to traumatic event.

Means for each subscale from intake to discharge and from discharge to three-month follow-up showed a consistent pattern of reduction of symptoms as follows:

CAQ SUBSCALE MEANS

	N	Intake	N	Discharge	N	3 Month
I. Re-experiencing	168	3.14	168	2.39	150	2.09
II. Avoidance	168	2.95	168	2.25	150	2.03
III. Arousal	168	3.12	168	2.46	150	2.23

Analysis of these means for each subscale was conducted at intake, discharge, and three-month follow-up utilizing ANOVA to identify between-group differences. All means were statistically different from each other at intake, discharge, and three-month follow-up. All alpha or p values exceeded 0.05.

ANOVA GROUP DIFFERENCE

	Mean Difference	**Significance**
I. Re-experiencing		
Intake to discharge	.7447	$p<0.001$
Discharge to follow-up	.3005	$p<0.001$
Intake to follow-up	1.045	$p<0.01$
II. Avoidance		
Intake to discharge	.7011	$p<.001$
Discharge to follow-up	.2193	$p<0.05$
Intake to follow-up	.9205	$p<0.001$
III. Arousal		
Intake to discharge	.6546	$p<0.001$
Discharge to follow-up	.2367	$p<0.05$
Intake to follow-up	.8914	$p<0.001$

Parent Questionnaire

The Parent Questionnaire was composed of 22 questions; there were no subscales. At intake the questionnaire captured parents observations of their child both before and after the trauma. The questionnaire was re-administered at discharge and three-month follow-up. At intake there were 143 questionnaires. Ten parents did not know of their foster child's behavior prior to the trauma, reducing the number of pre-trauma responses to 133. At discharge 145 questionnaires were available, and at three-month follow-up 143 were available. Averaged means showed a consistent pattern of reductions of parent-observed post trauma symptoms from intake to discharge and three-month follow-up. Three-month follow-up means showed that parents perceived their children's symptoms were only very slightly above the pre-trauma level as follows:

AVERAGE MEAN REDUCTION OF REACTIONS

	N	Average Means
Intake Pre-Trauma	133	2.14
Intake Post-Trauma	143	3.22
Discharge	145	2.50
Three-month follow-up	143	2.28

Analysis of these means was conducted at intake, discharge and three-month follow-up utilizing ANOVA to identify between-group differences. Means were significantly different from each other at intake and discharge. Although post-traumatic symptoms continued to ameliorate after discharge for the majority of children, a smaller number of children stayed the same or lost some of the gains made in treatment. Therefore the improvement between discharge and follow-up was not statistically significant at the 0.05 alpha level as follows:

ANOVA GROUP DIFFERENCES OF AVERAGE MEAN REDUCTION

	Mean Difference	Significance
Intake: Pre-trauma to Post-trauma	-1.07	$p<0.001$
Intake: Post-trauma to Discharge	.72	$p<0.001$
Discharge to Three-Month Follow-up	.21	$p<0.05$
Intake to Three-Month Follow-up	.93	$p<0.001$

ANALYSIS II
Matching Parent and Child/Adolescent Questionnaires

An analysis of the data collected was conducted to identify cases in which time series data was available for both child and parent. The analysis yielded 100 such cases. Demographics of these clients appear on the next page:

Demographics of Subjects
N=100

Gender	M	%	F	%	Not reported	%	Total
	42	42.0	56	56.0	2	2.0	100/100

Race/Ethnicity	White	%	Black	%	Hispanic	%	Other (non-white)	%	Total
	74	74.0	15	15.0	7	7.0	4	4.01	100/100

Psychosocial History of Subjects
N=100

	Yes	%	No	%	Not Reported	%	Total
Taking Psychotropic Medication	24	24.0	75	75.0	1	1.0	
Past Treatment by Mental Health Professional	32	32.0	67	67.0	1	1.0	
In Special Education Classes	24	24.0	74	74.0	2	2.0	
Experienced Trauma Prior to Most-Recent Trauma	63	63.0	30	30.0	7	7.0	

Child/Adolescent Questionnaire

For the children in this group (N=100) means at intake, discharge, and three-month follow-up appear in the chart below. Means for each subscale from intake to discharge and from discharge to follow-up shows a consistent pattern of reduction of symptoms as follows:

		Intake	Discharge	Follow-up
I.	Re-experiencing	3.19	2.39	2.12
II.	Avoidance	3.00	2.25	2.06
III.	Arousal	3.19	2.52	2.27

Analysis of these means for each subscale was conducted at intake, discharge, and three-month follow-up utilizing ANOVA to identify between group differences. Means were significantly different at intake and discharge indicating that PTSD symptoms had ameliorated between intake and discharge at a statistically significant level. However, although PTSD symptoms continued to ameliorate after discharge for the majority of children, a smaller number of children stayed the same or lost some of the gains made in treatment. Therefore the improvement between discharge and follow-up was not statistically significant at the 0.05 alpha level.

	Mean Difference	**Significance**
I. Re-experiencing		
Intake to discharge	.80	$p<0.001$
Discharge to follow-up	.27	$p<0.05$
Intake to follow-up	1.07	$p<0.001$
II. Avoidance		
Intake to discharge	.76	$p<0.001$
Discharge to follow-up	.19	$p<0.05$
Intake to follow-up	.94	$p<0.001$
III. Arousal		
Intake to discharge	.67	$p<0.001$
Discharge to follow-up	.25	$p<0.05$
Intake to follow-up	.92	$p<0.001$

Parent Questionnaire

Means demonstrate an amelioration of PTSD symptoms from intake to discharge and further amelioration of symptoms between discharge and three-month follow-up. At three-month follow-up parents perceived that their children's PTSD symptoms were only slightly higher than pre-trauma, as follows:

THREE MONTH FOLLOW-UP MEAN SCORES

	N	Mean Scores
Intake: Pre-trauma	93*	2.16
Intake: Post-trauma	99**	3.32
Discharge	100	2.53
Three-month follow-up	99***	2.29

*6 before trauma and 1 after trauma missing
**1 after trauma missing
***1 after trauma missing

An analysis of these means was conducted at intake, discharge, and three-month follow-up utilizing ANOVA to identify between group differences. Means were significantly different from each other between intake and discharge. However, although post traumatic stress symptoms continued to ameliorate for the majority of children, a smaller number of children stayed the same or lost some of the gains made in treatment. Therefore the improvement between discharge and follow-up was not significant at the 0.05 alpha level.

ANOVA IDENTIFIED GROUP DIFFERENCES

	Mean	Significance
Intake: Pre-trauma to post-trauma	-1.16	$p<0.001$
Intake: Post-trauma to discharge	.79	$p<0.001$
Discharge to three-month follow-up	.24	$p<0.05$
Intake to three-month follow-up	1.03	$p<0.001$

Multivariate Analysis

Multivariate quantitative analysis was used to describe participant's level of trauma as well as to assess the effectiveness of the intervention in reducing trauma levels after controlling for differences in age, gender, ethnicity, socioeconomic status, traumatic events, and time since traumatic event occurred. Linear regression models were utilized to predict each of the subscales at intake, discharge, and three-month follow-up as well as to run models predicting overall change in the three subscales (avoidance, arousal, re-experiencing).

Intake, Discharge, Three-Month Follow-Up

There were no significant predictors of subscale scores at time of intake. Gender, ethnicity, socio-economic status, type of traumatic incident and time since the onset of the incident were not significant predictors of overall change across the three subscales. Age at time of current trauma was a significant predictor of positive change (i.e. decrease in symptoms) for the arousal subscale (III) at discharge. It came close to attaining statistical significance of a predictor of positive change for the re-experiencing (I) and avoidance (II) subscales at discharge. Age at time of current trauma was not a significant predictor of positive change in any of the three subscales at three-month follow-up. However, it came close to attaining significance for the re-experiencing subscale (I) at that time.

This study documented that children experience severe levels of PTSD symptoms following non-assaultive, as well as, violent incidents. It further documented that levels of trauma continue to exist years after exposure without trauma-specific intervention. It demonstrated that use of the *Trauma Response Kit* (*Trauma Intervention Program: Short Term Intervention for Children and Adolescents*) by trained clinicians did, in fact, assist in the reduction of symptoms across all subcategories and, for most, continued that reduction three months after the last intervention. It demonstrated that the most severe (multiple traumas) saw the greatest reduction in reactions, contrary to the myth that little can be done to help those exposed to multiple traumas. Of the seven participants who saw an increase of reaction severity at the three-month follow-up, all had experienced additional traumas from the final session to the follow-up. Interestingly, their follow-up scores, although higher than final session scores, were not as high as the intake scores suggesting that coping skills learned in the intervention lessened the impact of these additional traumas. Findings also support immediate intervention with younger children who's physical, emotional, social level of vulnerability may be more at risk than older children.

The *Trauma Response Intervention Program* is now an integral part of the SITCAP strategies and continues to assist children and their families as documented by ongoing anecdotal accounts from the Institute's Certified Trauma and Loss Consultants and Specialists across the country. Additional research also continues on the relationship of variables to severity and intervention outcomes.

CHAPTER SIX
Overview
***Structured Sensory Intervention for Traumatized Children,
Adolescents & Parents (SITCAP)***

Earlier chapters detailed the theoretical foundations of The National Institute for Trauma and Loss in Children's SITCAP intervention model. Reliving the incident (exposure), telling the story (trauma narrative), and reordering the experience in a way that is manageable (cognitive reframing) were identified as the primary intervention strategies. The structure in which these strategies are initiated is critical to maintaining a sense of safety while actively involving the child, adolescent or parent in the healing process.

The Structure

SITCAP is structured because with structure comes a sense of control and safety. After the second session the victim/survivor knows how to respond, and what to expect. He gets comfortable with the predictability of the process. The structure is also a benefit for the trauma intervenor. It provides direction; where to go next, what to do, what to say. It also affords the intervenor the same sense of safety and control. Most importantly it keeps the intervenor in the role of witness versus clinician. Victims desperately want to, and are capable of, sharing the details of their experience - to make us a witness to that experience. To be a witness, we must be involved in the child's telling of the story by being curious about all that happened. To engage this "witness" role, the intervenor must be very concrete and literal in response to all the elements of the story, it's details and the visual representations provided by the child, adolescent or parent. If the intervenor attempts to make sense of the child's emotional status by analyzing "why", he will not be able to experience the trauma as the child is experiencing it. He will not "know it" as the child knows it, and the child, adolescent or parent will not experience the intervenor as a witness, as someone who is with him in his experience. He will sense he is alone and shut down to protect himself.

SITCAP's structure also places boundaries on the intervenor as well as the victim. Part of becoming a witness is seeing how the victim now views himself and the world around him following the trauma. To see what the victim sees is to understand and know what will be helpful. Because trauma is a sensory experience the memory is often stored symbolically. Images - how one looks at himself and the world around him - defines what that trauma was like. Even adults rarely have words to adequately describe what their experience was like, but they can show us. Presenting that visual representation must be done in a structured fashion. Boundaries provide the structure which promotes a "sensory" safety. Boundaries in drawing involve the use of only 8 1/2" x 11" paper and fine point, color pencils or felt markers. Drawing activities are structured versus unstructured. They direct themselves to helping the victim describe how specific sensations or themes of trauma like fear, revenge, hurt are now impacting his life.

Focus On Themes, Not Behavior

SITCAP focuses on ten major sensations or themes: fear, terror, worry, hurt, anger, revenge, accountability, safety, power and throughout the process shifting from victim thinking to survivor thinking. This process, therefore, does not direct itself to attempting to treat behavior but rather the sensations (themes) that fuel and drive the behavior. One seven year old boy, for example, at age three saw his father kill his mother. He was later kidnapped by his father who had posted bail. For the next six months he was held captive by his father. He was left alone for long periods of time and witnessed his father beat several women. There was a four year period from the time this boy was rescued to the time SITCAP was initiated. During that time two primary behaviors resulting from his trauma surfaced. The first was that he slept on the floor every night and the second was he would seldom leave his grandmother's side. He would even follow her into the bathroom at times making it difficult for her to have any privacy without a struggle.

Sleeping on the floor was a way of being in a state of readiness for any danger that might come his way. Following his grandmother into the bathroom was rooted in the sensation of fear. His behaviors were helping, at a sensory level, to create the sensation of safety. SITCAP did not directly address this boy's behavior, but his fears and worries. By helping him re-experience the sensation of safety, his levels of fear and worry were reduced and the behavior changed. Following the restoration of the sense of safety, he began to cognitively alter his responses.

In another example, Robert, an eleven year old boy was facing his second suspension from school for fighting. One year earlier his older sister was brutally raped and murdered by a serial killer. He was not a witness to the killing, but was certainly traumatized by his sister's murder and all the exposure from the media that followed. Fighting had not previously been a problem. His mother reported that it was totally unlike her son.

Attempts at peer mediation and conflict resolution which frequently focus on behavior and seek resolution through cognitive approaches simply failed. At a sensory level, this youngster was terrified. His "fighting response" was an attempt, at a sensory level, to not feel afraid. It was a way for him to overpower his fear; to communicate to others and to himself, "No one is going to do to me what was done to my sister." SITCAP helped him to "recapture", at a sensory level, a sense of power and safety that helped diminish the fighting response. Help the victim with the sensations of trauma and behavior will change accordingly.

Details

Part of telling the story is asking questions to elicit details. Obtaining details is another very important component of the SITCAP process. For the victim, details can provide a sense of control as well as a sense of relief. For the intervenor, details can point the way to helping the client find relief.

When asked where he felt the hurt the most, Robert, the eleven year old boy whose sister was brutally murdered one year earlier, said, "All over my body when I was told. It was like I was in shock and then I got a big headache." He continued to experience the headaches when he thought of his sister. While pursuing this with him he told the story of how, on the same night his sister was discovered missing, his friend was in a car accident. His friend's head went through the windshield, and he died. Given the high profile of the murder, no one ever dealt with this second traumatization that seemed minimal compared to the murder. Only by providing Robert the opportunity to tell the entire story and all the details of what happened at the time of the incident did this second trauma reveal itself as a source of some of the headaches he was experiencing. He in essence had two stories to tell. All too often, it is the events following the primary trauma that trigger trauma reactions.

The structure of SITCAP keeps the intervenor and child focused on details as a way of being able to later "see" the experience differently, to cognitively reframe it in a way that is now manageable. Details also can provide information that helps to make sense out of what happened and may still be happening with the child.

Education

Structuring statements at intake clearly identify how the process works, what will be expected and what outcome can be anticipated. The time devoted to "structuring" the SITCAP process helps to reduce anxiety. It also helps victims to make an informed consent. All too often the counselors simply move directly into treatment without addressing the implications for the client. The client is not prepared to really confirm, "Yes, this is what I want." SITCAP uses specific resource materials for this educational component to ensure the child has some sense of what he is about to experience as well as learn.

SITCAP also structures itself to teach the victim the difference between grief and trauma. If a loved one was undergoing surgery and the doctor told you he would meet with you in the surgical waiting room when the operation was completed at 3 p.m., and if at 3:15 p.m. the doctor had not yet shown up, you would panic. You would begin to think the worst. What you need more than anything else to calm your anxiety is information. A trauma victim's needs are no different. Information about trauma lessens anxiety. Normalizing trauma reactions helps to make sense out of what happened while supporting the fact that what is being experienced is quite normal. This helps to decrease anxiety.

Grief and Trauma

Not everyone who experiences grief will experience trauma, but everyone who experience a trauma will also experience grief. However, trauma is so overpowering that it often "buries" grief reactions. Once a victim is helped to find relief from the terror of their trauma and reexperiences a renewed sense of power, buried grief reactions often emerge. In reality, one is often dealing with grief and trauma simultaneously. The focus of intervention therefore must address both. SITCAP structures it's activities to respond to grief and trauma.

Type of Incidents

SITCAP addresses Type I and Type II incidents (Terr 1991). Type I refers to a single trauma-inducing incident. Type II trauma refers to a single incident, like sexual abuse, repeated over a chronic period of time, or multiple traumas (different incidents). By addressing the major themes of trauma SITCAP is beneficial for both Type I and Type II incidents. It addresses those incidents that are assaultive and violent, such as murder, physical/sexual abuse, domestic violence, armed assault and suicide. It also addresses incidents of a non-assaultive origin, such as terminal illness, critical injury, natural disasters, car fatalities, house fires, drownings, divorce or separation from parents.

Age, Gender, Ethnicity

It is important to remember that trauma has very few boundaries when it comes to culture, ethnicity, gender or age. Whatever an adult can experience in trauma, a child can also experience. Whatever a child can experience in trauma, an adult can also experience.

A twenty-seven year old woman's brother was shot and killed just outside her home. As she tells her story, she describes hearing the gun shot and immediately knowing it was her brother who was shot. He was a random victim in this case.

There was no gang or drug history. When she ran outside her fear was confirmed. She said that as she approached his body she wanted to touch him, but she knew if she "touched him he would die." She could not touch him.

This woman's response is an example of "magical thinking". Magical thinking is a reaction generally assigned to young children who believe it was something they thought, said, or wished for, that was the cause of death of a family member or friend. Whatever a child can experience, however, an adult in trauma can experience. A forty-two year old nurse's teenage son was shot and killed outside her home. Telling her story, she talks about looking at that spot twenty-four hours a day. She goes on to say that at times she's cooking something on the stove and forgets she's cooking. The close physical proximity to the trauma, among other elements, has kept her in the hyperarousal state. Forgetting she is cooking is a short-term memory loss associated with the mid-brain arousal response that is experienced by children as well as adults. It manifests itself in traumatized children who seem "not to be listening" because they cannot remember what they were asked to do just five minutes earlier.

SITCAP intervention adjusts activities for developmental differences, but its focus on major sensations or themes versus behavior allows it to help reduce symptoms across age levels. It's primary intervention processes of exposure, trauma narrative and cognitive reframing, remain the processes for pre-school aged children, elementary aged children, adolescents and adults.

Structured Sensory Intervention is unique in several ways.
- Intervention can be initiated for either violent or non-violent trauma incidents of the type detailed earlier.
- Intervention addresses children of pre-school age, children 6 - 12 years old, adolescents and adults.
- Activity worksheets accompany each session and are designed to facilitate focus on the major themes of trauma.
- The interventions are so structured, trauma-focused and client-oriented that clinicians who follow the format are afforded little opportunity to inappropriately respond.
- Field-tested in schools as well as agency settings, the model and its interventions meet the many limitations placed on school counselors, social workers and clinicians.

- Rather than address symptoms, the model focuses on the themes of trauma -- fear, terror, worry, hurt, anger, revenge, accountability, safety, power and being a survivor versus a victim.
- Given the reality that parental involvement is frequently minimal, the model encourages a minimum of two sessions with parents. These are specifically structured and designed to obtain necessary information and support, and to provide the opportunity to make the parent a witness to the ways the trauma has impacted the child so as to increase the likelihood that parental response to the child is the most supportive.
- The parent component also addresses those parents whose child's trauma has triggered reactions from their own person history or parents who themselves suffer a trauma not involving their child, but creating problems for them in their role as a parent.
- Exposure is accomplished by drawing activities. Developing the trauma narrative is accomplished through asking trauma-specific questions, and cognitive reframing is structured to speak to the major sensations of trauma.
- Resource materials for the child/parent ensure that they receive the information (education) they need about the differences between grief and trauma as well as the course the intervention will take. These are also included in a structured booklet format to ensure that the intervenors are, in fact, covering the important issues.
- The model is outcome driven. An assessment tool is available to identify current reactions and their severity levels. It provides a baseline to compare initial levels of severity to final outcomes. It is clinically based, so it serves as a diagnostic tool to support third party insurance requirements for approved treatment and if needed, continuation beyond the short-term period.
- The components of SITCAP are also designed to assist school/community's response to critical incidents. In school environments, school shootings, car fatalities, and sudden death of staff dictate a specific series of interventions from the first day through several weeks. The SITCAP model provides these interventions. (Detailed in Chapter Nine, Debriefing.)

Eight to Ten Sessions

Structured Sensory Intervention for Traumatized Children, Adolescents and Parents is an eight to ten session intervention. The attention of pre-school aged children varies from fifteen to twenty-five minutes. It therefore takes ten sessions to cover the major themes of trauma for that age group. Children, adolescents and adult/parent intervention involves eight structured sessions which address the major themes of trauma in a sequential manner. Activities vary to some degree with different age levels, but the primary intervention processes and focus on major trauma sensations and themes are used with all age levels.

Participants in SITCAP may not need all eight sessions as levels of severity and reactions will vary. Some participants may need additional intervention. SITCAP lends itself to identifying those reactions (themes) that may need additional attention. Additional intervention, if needed, can therefore be very focused and specific to the client's needs. Overall reactions, for example, may see a reduction but safety remains a primary worry. Additional intervention would then concentrate on safety issues. Some individuals may also see major reductions in all three DSM-IV subcategories, yet need "first aid" following additional exposure or when entering different developmental periods.

The goals of SITCAP are:
- Stabilization (return to previous level of functioning or prevention of further dysfunction).
- Identification of PTSD reactions;
- The opportunity to revisit the trauma in the supportive, reassuring presence of an adult (professional) who understands the value of providing this opportunity.
- An opportunity to find relief from trauma-induced terror, worry, hurt, anger, revenge, accountability, powerlessness, and the need for safety;
- An opportunity to re-establish a positive "connectiveness" to the adult world;
- Normalization of current and future reactions;
- Support of the heroic efforts to become a survivor rather than a victim of their experience;

- When appropriate, assistance for parents in resolving those reactions triggered by their child's traumatization;
- Replacement of the traumatic sensory experience with positive sensory experiences;
- Identification of additional needs and recognition of the role parents can take to help meet those needs;
- The provisioning of parents with ways to respond to their traumatized child's reactions.

Drawing

Although discussed in earlier chapters, the importance of drawing in accomplishing these goals bears reviewing as drawing itself is a major component of SITCAP.

- Drawing is a psychomotor activity. Because trauma is a sensory experience, not a cognitive experience, intervention is necessary to trigger those sensory memories. Drawing triggers those sensory memories when it is trauma focused. It provides a safe vehicle to communicate what children, even adults, often have few words to describe.
- Drawing engages the child/adult in the active involvement with their own healing. It takes them from a passive to an active, directed, controlled externalization of that trauma and its reactions.
- Drawing provides a symbolic representation of the trauma experience in a format that is now external, concrete, and therefore manageable. The paper acts as a container of that trauma.
- Drawing provides a visual focus on details that encourage the client via trauma-specific questions, to tell his story, to give it a language so it can be reordered in a way that is manageable.
- Drawing also provides for the diminishing of reactivity (anxiety) to trauma memories through repeated visual reexposure in a medium that is perceived and felt by the client to be safe.

Trauma-specific Questions

In addition to drawing, trauma-specific questions are used to help in the telling of the story and detailing with reactions experienced.

Questions are directed to trauma themes and focus on trauma sensations, and are also directed to the details of the trauma incident itself. Following are some examples:

- "What do you remember seeing or hearing?" relates to the overall sensory imploding of detailed components of the trauma.
- "Do you sometimes think about what happened even when you don't want to?" deals with intrusive thoughts.
- "Do certain sounds, sights, smells, etc, sometimes suddenly remind you of what happened?" refers to startle reactions.
- "What would you like to see happen to the person (or thing) that caused this to happen?" deals with anger and revenge.
- " Do you sometimes think it should have been you instead?" is an accountability (survivor guilt) question.

Throughout the process, questions are specific to the theme being addressed. Their concreteness keeps the child focused on the specific theme, encourages the narrative (story) to be told for each theme, and encourages the attention to detail. Details, as discussed earlier, are critical to helping establish a sense of control and provide the intervenor with information needed to help the child find relief.

Multiple questions are asked because the specific trauma reference may be worry, not anger or revenge. The child's trauma reference may be about the hurt experienced at a sensory level not the physical level. It may be accountability for some, fear for others. SITCAP encourages the systematic presentation of all questions and attention to all themes to give the victim the opportunity to make us a witness to his specific trauma reference.

Example

It was New Year's Eve. A high school senior was ushering at a movie complex where several movies ran concurrently. He was slated to graduate in the spring and had been accepted into the police academy. Also a football player, he was physically quite strong and stood over six feet tall. Several kids in the movie he was assigned to were causing trouble. He attempted to get control but was unable to do so. He sought out the manager for help, but the manager had a full house and told him he would just have to handle it on his own. The situation did not change. In this complex, movies were scheduled so several let out at the same time. There was a "common" area that the theatres opened into, so everyone was moving into this area simultaneously. The youngster took his post across the common area outside the doors of the movie he was responsible to monitor. When the youths he had trouble with came out of the movie and into the common area they spotted him, rushed him, knocked him down and began beating on him. They broke his nose and several ribs. About a month later his parish priest, who was trying to help this youngster, called for assistance. The boy was skipping school and not attending the youth activities at church, which was not at all like him.

"What was the worst part for you?" was one of the trauma-specific questions that helped to encourage this youngster's telling of the story and focusing on specific details. When this case was presented in trainings and participants were asked to anticipate what the "worst part" must have been, their numerous responses rarely identified what the worst part was for this teenager. Responses ranged from the anger he felt at the manager for leaving him on his own, the embarrassment and shame that he couldn't help himself and the pain he felt during the beating. The point is, what we often as observers consider to be the worst part is not necessarily experienced by the victim. Only by giving the victim the opportunity to make us a witness can we truly know his experience as he knows it.

The teen's response was as follows:

"I can see it as if it is happening all over again. I'm on the ground and they're kicking me. As they are kicking me I can see between their legs. (This kind of detail is unique to trauma in which events seem to happen almost in slow motion so that such details emerge.) As I'm looking between their legs, I see all these people standing around and no one is helping me."

At that moment in time, he experienced complete abandonment, betrayed by the adults in his world. Without appropriate intervention this could have easily triggered very self-defeating, even destructive responses. He had already begun to isolate himself, was missing school and was putting his future in jeopardy. If he had gone much longer without help, it would not have been unusual for him to start carrying a weapon, join a gang, or even actively seek out the kids who beat him with the intent of getting revenge. Being unable to trust the adult world was the worst part of his experience and one that often leads to destructive behavior and identifying with the aggressor.

By asking this one trauma-specific question, the specialist was able to help this teen work through the abandonment he experienced; a focus that likely would have otherwise gone untreated.

Cognitive Reframing

Cognitive reframing is scripted in SITCAP to insure that the victim is provided a "survivors" way of making sense of the trauma experience. The goal is to help move the victim from "victim thinking" to "survivor thinking" which leads to empowerment, choice, active involvement in their own healing process and a renewed sense of safety and hope.

Activities also assist in supporting the reframing of the experience. The high school senior, in our earlier example, who was beaten on New Year's Eve and had lost trust in the adult world, withdrew. By having him draw what his fears looked like and later giving them a name, he realized he was responding as a victim to his own fear that, if the police academy found out, they would never allow him to start his training. This was irrational, but not from a "victim's" viewpoint. A sense of shame also emerged as his view of self was not being able to take care of himself. When asked why standard operating procedure of police was to always work with a partner, he was able to refocus on the reality that alone, even in the midst of bystanders, protection and help was not always given. Working in pairs, he realized, dealt with the reality that even the police could find themselves suddenly overwhelmed. At a cognitive level, he was then able to reframe that what happened to him was not his fault and that as a police officer he would be doing for others what others could not do for him - help. In this sense, cognitive framing allowed him to reorder his experience in a way that gave his future new meaning.

Parent Involvement

A good deal of research has concluded that parents are critical to their child's ability to recover from trauma. Pynoos and Nader (1988) and Vogel and Verberg (1993) cited parents as the single most important support for school age children following a disaster. Byers (1996) reported that studies following World War II showed that the level of upset displayed by the adult in the child's life, not the war itself, was the single most important factor in predicting the emotional well being and recovery of the child. We see the same relationship today.

An unstable parent creates an unstable child. A traumatized adult will find it difficult to help their traumatized child. Schwarz (1991) and many others have found that adults (parents), more frequently than children, experienced the greatest distress when presented with a trauma. van der Kolk (1996) wrote "most children are amazingly resilient as long as they have caregivers that are emotionally available."

When a child has been traumatized, his parents also experience extreme distress and often are unable to adequately respond to their traumatized children without appropriate intervention.

Learning about trauma helps parents who themselves have been traumatized, especially when their experience is brought back to life (triggered) by their child's traumatic experience. Education is an essential, necessary component to help the parent become aware of how her own unresolved fears block her ability to allow her child to openly tell his story. The child needs a parent who is not terrified and emotionally overwhelmed. Parents with their own history often discover that their child's experience threatens to bring all the terror of their own experience back to life. Unknowingly, they reject their child's cry for help, or minimize the child's terror in hopes of calming the child.

Given the reality that parent involvement in intervention can be minimal, two sessions with parents can still support significant reduction of trauma reactions in their children. This is especially the case if those sessions are structured and focused on helping the parent become "a witness" to their child's experience as well.

Parents generally underestimate the impact trauma has on their children. This is partially due to not understanding how trauma is different than grief and how it manifests itself in children. Therefore, parents need to be educated. Furthermore, until a parent can experience what the child has experienced, it is difficult for her to understand and accept recommendations as to how she needs to respond differently to her child. Deblinger, Lippman, & Steer (1996) conducted a very structured intervention with parents and children who were sexually abused. Exposure, developing the trauma narrative, and cognitive restructuring were the primary interventions. Of most importance was the finding related to parental involvement; the greatest reductions were seen in those cases where parents participated in the intervention. Children seen without the parent did not realize the same gains.

However, the intervention must be structured. The purpose of the first session with the parent is to obtain factual information about the trauma and to identify changes in the child's behavior, mood, emotions, relationships, and performance since the trauma. The parent also needs to learn what trauma is and the ways she can be helpful during the intervention process. This information should be in written form as it must be seen as well as heard.

The assumption is that the professional leading the intervention will have been trained in the differences between grief and trauma and can be very concrete and specific in the description of trauma to parents. Appropriate trauma-specific intervention cannot be provided by the professional who cannot identify the five major differences between grief and trauma, provide explicit examples for each of the trauma-specific reactions as classified in the DSM-IV, nor review the ten major themes of trauma with the parent. This is the type of information learned and practiced in training at the Institute.

The second session with the parent comes only after the child has had the several sessions needed to construct the trauma narrative and can provide visual representations (drawings) of how that experience has impacted him. This would take place at the seventh session when using the SITCAP model. In that seventh session, the child will use his drawings to tell his story. The parent should be allowed to be a witness to this experience just as the professional has been over the sessions leading up to this meeting with the parent. This is a very critical and pivotal session. It is an opportunity to reconnect the child's trust in his parent; to relate to the parent as someone who understands (as the professional does). It is an opportunity for the parent to become a witness, to appreciate the need to respond differently to her child, affording her child the sense of safety and protection so desperately needed to become a survivor.

In the example of the seven year old boy who slept on the floor for fear of falling asleep in bed and followed his grandmother into the bathroom, he had never been given the opportunity to make his grandmother a witness to his experience. She knew her grandson had been terribly traumatized, yet at a sensory level did not really "know". Her standard response to him following her into the bathroom and sleeping on the floor was, "You're a big boy now. Seven year olds do not follow their grandma into the bathroom." This was a predictable response, as was her frustration with him at times.

Others had told her to be patient, that it would take time for him to get over this. She didn't understand this because she was not a witness to how the murder had impacted her grandson. No one had involved this youngster in trauma-specific drawings or the pursuit of trauma themes. He did not really have a way to tell his mother until he was involved in SITCAP. It was only when grandmother became a witness that she really "knew" and could thereafter respond differently.

When asked to draw a picture of what happened to his mother (Plate 1) he drew his father with a gun, the bullet in the middle of the air, mom in the direction of the oncoming bullet. He drew himself standing next to mom.

When asked to tell what happened, he replied, "My dad, he be's mean to my mom. She was happy because she was going to move out of the house to my grandma's. She went out to the car and when she came back to get me, because she forgot me, then my dad shot her. The police then came and got my dad."

Plate 1

Grandmother had never heard this story. It doesn't matter whether it's real - it is what is driving his behavior. In three years of therapy no one had ever asked him to draw a picture of what happened. No one ever asked him to draw a picture of his mother dead, nor asked the kinds of trauma questions asked in this interview. Within a few short minutes of the beginning of an hour-long telling of the story, grandmother quickly came to know his fear, his terror of being left alone. If we had attempted through the traditional approach of suggesting to her ways to respond differently, they would have been difficult for her to accept. Experiencing his trauma at a sensory level, seeing it as he saw it, helped her to know his need for safety and reassurance as well as know how to provide that reassurance on those days he was feeling vulnerable and powerless.

Levels of Parent Involvement

There are three possible levels of parent involvement with trauma. At the first level a parent's child has been traumatized, and the parent needs assistance to understand what trauma is, how it is different from grief and the ways she can best help her child recover. To accomplish this, the parent needs to learn about trauma, the process of intervention, and then be a witness to her child's trauma through the child's telling of the story with drawings in the same way he made the intervenor a witness. This can be accomplished in two sessions: at intake and then again after the child has completed SITCAP intervention which could be completed in as few as two sessions or as many as eight.

The second level deals with the parent whose child has been traumatized, and that trauma triggers memories and reactions of the parent's own past personal experience with trauma. The triggering of these trauma-related reactions frequently prevents the parent from appropriately attending to the child's specific trauma needs. The child's fears trigger the parent's fears. Predictably, parents often shut down to protect themselves; to get control of their own fears. These parents need the opportunity to address their trauma issues with the goal of helping them "be there" for their child. This can often be accomplished in two sessions (in addition to the regular sessions directed at helping the child). In some cases the parent's trauma may necessitate intervention of a level three nature.

At level three the parent has suffered a trauma, but not the child. The parent's trauma is likely to get in the way of functioning as a parent to the child and also disrupt the relationship with the spouse. The same major themes addressed with children and adolescents are addressed with the adult. Drawing remains a primary activity along with telling the story and cognitive reframing.

An additional focus with level three parents is secondary wounding. Secondary wounding refers to the responses from others following the trauma, especially those in the position of helpers. "At least you're alive." "You're young, you'll get over it." "It really couldn't have happened that way. You're over reacting." "If only you would have ____." These responses do wound. Often victims report that the wounding suffered after the trauma is worse and harder to get past than the actual trauma. Secondary wounding can occur with reactions of denial and disbelief, discounting and minimizing, blaming, treating one as defective, and through system victimization. Structured intervention for parents addresses these issues and provides the education and treatment to help parents help themselves and help their children. The parent intervention process is detailed in Chapter Eight.

SITCAP and Schools

Schools have special needs following trauma-inducing, critical incidents. The school environment itself is quite unique. Interventions provided in the community are not always easily adaptable to the uniqueness of the school environment and its population. Varied developmental levels and special populations necessitate interventions comprehensive enough to meet these varied needs. The administration of a school also presents unique functions that interventions must take into consideration.

The SITCAP model provides a comprehensive series of trauma debriefing interventions specifically for schools, students, staff and administration. Trauma debriefing intervention includes the following interventions. Debriefing for the adolescent and adult population, defusing for younger children, operational debriefing for all staff, crisis team debriefing for school crisis team members, and the classroom presentation are the varied interventions needed and structured by SITCAP.

Each of the trauma debriefing interventions are described in Chapter Nine - Debriefing. The stages of each of these models are detailed in *Trauma Debriefing Handbook for Schools and Agencies* (Steele, 1999). The Handbook provides step by step movement through each process and provides the support material considered a necessary component for helping schools heal from their trauma. These interventions are designed to accelerate the healing process and prevent future PTSD reactions. However, for some, especially the most exposed, additional intervention is often needed. The transition into the children and adolescent programs within the SITCAP model provide the interventions that debriefing cannot provide.

Detailed Intervention Practices

The SITCAP model provides very structured, sensory focused interventions for pre-school children three to six years, children six to twelve years and adolescents thirteen to eighteen years. This model incorporates the notion that major sensations following trauma inducement are common to each age group. Fear, worry, hurt, anger, revenge, accountability, safety, power and survivor versus victim thinking and behavior are experienced at a sensory level. When these reactions are incomplete or "frozen" in the trauma state, the "completion" of these responses to trauma must be discharged at a sensory level in order to restore balance to the child (Levine, 1996).

The intervention activities used to restore balance to the traumatized child are, as detailed earlier, based upon exposure through drawing, trauma narrative through trauma-specific questions directed to the major sensations experienced and specific questions to elicit the details of the story developed by the child and cognitive reframing. Although the activities vary to appropriately fit the developmental levels of the children, the process and focus remains the same for each age group. Practitioners will be able to initiate and integrate this process into practice but caution is still urged and training recommended as any process is best experienced before using. As safety is of major concern in treating traumatized children, such caution is believed, by the authors, to be a responsibility.

The detailing of each individual session for the three different groups would be far too extensive for this text. Each program is a book in itself. However, by providing examples of how the different sensations are approached with each age group, an understanding will be established for the process and its value, which are documented by research and field testing.

There are several areas that do not change regardless of the age of the child. As stated, the trauma sensations addressed are the same. These sensations are also referred to as the themes of trauma. A specific sensation can run through the child's reaction to his experience and appear as a "theme". The requested number of visits and focus of parental involvement in intervention is the same. Each program uses activity worksheets that are titled according to the theme being addressed. *This is What Happened,* is one activity worksheet, for example, used with each age group. The focus on developing survivor thinking and behavior is common also to each age group. The programs are short term, running an average of eight sessions. The pre-school program has ten sessions simply because the concentration span of pre-school children is shorter, as are the sessions for the preschool children. All programs have been field tested in school settings as well as agency settings to ensure they work within the parameters and needs of these two settings.

CHAPTER SEVEN
Beginning the Intervention:
Focus and Strategies of Sessions

Parental involvement is critical to outcome, yet obtaining parental involvement often meets with numerous barriers, some avoidable, others in part due to the dysfunction of parents. The SITCAP model therefore initially limits the time involvement, yet structures sessions with parents to maximize that involvement. The time and interaction with the parents is the same for all three programs. When parents are open to additional assistance in helping their child or, in the case of their own trauma, helping themselves, the SITCAP model includes trauma-specific interventions which are detailed in Chapter Eight.

A brief description of the initial parental involvement is presented here to address issues that are important to understand and to be prepared for, before initiating intervention with the child. This will then be followed by case examples of the intervention activities used to address the major themes of trauma.

Attendance at a minimum of two sessions is requested of parents. These sessions include the intake session and a parent-child session structured to help make the parent a witness to how the trauma has impacted her child in a way similar to how the intervenor has become a witness. A session following the initial session with the child is optional and used to give the parent feedback about the child's evaluation results and status. Most parents will schedule this session. Some will be open to the presentation by phone, if it is not possible for them to attend.

Parents who have had a previous history of trauma and are now reexperiencing that trauma because of their child's trauma, or they themselves have been traumatized recently, can find help through additional sessions available through the parent component of the SITCAP model.

Intake Session

The intake session seeks detailed information about the traumatic incident, history related factors that may have increased the child's vulnerability at exposure, and a description of the child's behaviors, moods, relationships and learning factors prior to the trauma and since the trauma. Of equal importance at this intake session is the education of the parent as to the differences between grief and trauma, the possible needs of their traumatized child, a description of the actual intervention process and, finally, a commitment from the parent to attend the parent-child session when the child tells his/her story to the parent.

Optional Follow-Up Session

The optional session follows the initial session with the child. The purpose of this parent session is to review the results of the PTSD Child/Adolescent Questionnaire and to answer any questions from the parent. This review often gives the parent a different understanding of the way in which her child has been impacted by the trauma. It helps increase awareness as to those trauma reactions present and holding the child "hostage" but, at the same time, not outwardly observable. Intrusive recollections, for example, can be very disturbing and disruptive. Intrusive recollections induce anxiety and can make it difficult to concentrate and focus, which can lead to additional performance problems especially in the school environment. However, intrusiveness is not generally observable. This type of educating of the parent helps the parent begin to "make sense" of her traumatized child's changes following exposure. If not already revealed, this session provides the parent the opportunity to acknowledge her own personal history with trauma. Possible placement in the parent program is then determined at this time.

Parent-Child Session

The parent-child session is critical. This session is designed to give the child/adolescent the opportunity to make his parent a witness to the way his trauma has been experienced. The child does this in the same way he does with the intervenor - telling his story with the use of his drawings and addressing the major sensations or themes of trauma. In this session the parent frequently experiences what the child experienced at the sensory level. The parent then comes to "know" the trauma in the same way her child "knows" what the experience was like.

This process can bring about almost immediate changes in the way parents respond to their traumatized children. What was before referred to by parents as "stubbornness", is now "known" as fear. What was referred to as "immature behavior" is now seen as a need for safety. This new understanding of the child's responses to trauma often allows the parent to also "know" how she needs to respond differently to her child. Instead of "I know you can do this", the parent intuitively understands and responds, "It must upset you that things you did so easily before what happened are so hard for you now."

It is important to keep in mind that the needs of parents following the traumatization of a child are unique. If these needs are not addressed from a trauma perspective and with a sensitivity to what can help alleviate parental anxiety, parental involvement is not likely to be supportive. The parent component addresses these needs and structures intervention to reduce, not increase parent anxiety.

The future use of "child" will refer to all ages, three through eighteen. Examples will identify the specific age of the child. The order of intervention is sequential. Following are the focal points of each session.

Session One

- Session one focuses on structuring the process for the child, educating, providing the opportunity to tell the story, what happened, what the victim looked like, normalization of reactions, identification of present trauma reactions and level of severity. In the first session educating the child as to what trauma is, how most react and what helps, is the beginning of cognitively reframing the child's view of what happened and has been happening to him since the trauma. In addition the child is informed of the ways this intervention can help. Booklets are used for each level of this education and cognitive reframing.

Session Two

- Session two addresses fear and worry. Two sessions are used to first identify and then defuse the feelings of traumatized preschool children. Preschool children, for example, will need help to identify what is meant by "hurt." A number of educational sensory activities are used to help the child.

Session Three

- This session addresses hurt, both physical and emotional. A good deal of effort is directed at where in the body the hurt was experienced and continues to be experienced.

Session Four

- Session four explores anger, revenge, accountability. Each of these sensations is rooted in powerlessness. Activities are designed to help children regain a renewed sense of power over themselves and the world around them.

Session Five

- In this session future orientation is the focus. This session focuses on survivor thinking as a way of finding relief from the sense of hopelessness and powerlessness created by trauma.

Session Six

- This is an important session that prepares the child for meeting with the parent. This session guides the child as to how to tell his story.

Session Seven

- Session seven is the parent-child meeting. The child tells his story using his drawings. This session is critical to re-connecting the child to the parent and to helping the child experience the parent as a witness.

Session Eight

- This final session is for a final review and reordering of the experience in a way that is now manageable. It is for re-administering the assessment tool to validate reductions in severity and/or support the need for additional intervention.

It is critical to keep in mind that throughout this process activities are designed to be safe and used to experience a renewed "sensation" of safety and empowerment. Furthermore activities, inclusive of drawing and cognitive reframing, are used to help the child move from victim thinking and behavior to survivor thinking and behavior.

Although stated earlier, this warrants repeating. The structured sensory experiences provided in this process together with giving the experience a "language" (trauma narrative) and helping the child now cognitively reframe his experience are the core elements of healing. It is the child's active involvement in his own healing process that initiates healing, not the intervenors insights, understanding, or analysis.

It is difficult for clinicians to stop the analysis and the attempts at insight. It is difficult for them to initially let the child tell his story. They want to reflect, explore and interpret feelings that take the child away from his story. It is almost as if the clinician wants to write the story for the child. For years, counseling programs in schools have taught students that it takes time to establish "rapport", that you cannot in the first session ask a child to draw a picture of the person who died, was killed or critically injured. This might be safer for the clinician but these children are living with their trauma daily and desperately wanting someone to give them an opportunity to make them a witness to their experience, to be there with them. Exposure through drawing and trauma-specific questions associated with the themes of trauma allow this to happen very quickly, yet safely.

This is by far the most difficult component for intervenors to accept. The acceptance generally doesn't come until they themselves experience the process at a sensory level when examining their own personal experience with loss or trauma. It is firmly accepted, as they begin to see the relief in the children whom they give the opportunity to tell their story, to make them a witness to it.

The objectives of the SITCAP components for children are:
1) To stabilize;
2) To identify intervention needs; PTSD reactions and short and long term goals;
3) To provide an opportunity to revisit the trauma in the supportive, reassuring presence of an adult (professional) who understands the value of providing this opportunity;
4) To provide an opportunity to find relief at a sensory level;
5) To provide an opportunity to reestablish a positive "connectiveness" to life;
6) To normalize current and future reactions;
7) To support the child's heroic efforts to become a survivor, not a victim of his experience;
8) To replace the child's trauma sensory experience, with a positive experience;
9) To identify additional needs and the role parents can take to help meet these needs.

At a sensory level the effort is focused on actively involving the child in his own healing process by providing the opportunity to:
1) Focus on internal resources;

2) Re-work the experience;
3) Experience a positive connectiveness to themselves (their bodies); something usually lost in a traumatic event;
4) Experience some relief in the process thereby encouraging continuation of the healing process;
5) Experience at a sensory level the power and hope inherent in seeing themselves as survivors.

The Child's First Session:
Educating and Normalizing

In the initial session it is important to educate the child as to what trauma is, how others respond to trauma, how intervention works and the ways it can help. Booklets are used in this process as it is easier to "show" than just "tell".

Brave Bart is used for preschool and early elementary children. *Brave Bart* is a story about a kitten (plate 1.1) who is traumatized and how he becomes a survivor with the help of Helping Hannah (plate 1.2), a neighborhood cat. It is written generically so children exposed to a variety of trauma-inducing incidents can relate to the story. It identifies trauma reactions and then tells how Brave Bart was helped.

Plate 1.1   Plate 1.2

The book tells and illustrates the many different reactions Brave Bart has had since the "very bad, sad, scary thing happened"; his fears, worries, confusions (plates 1.3, 1.4, 1.5). The story illustrates how things begin to change with Helping Hannah's help. She teaches him that what happened to him was a trauma and has him draw pictures of what happened (plate 1.6). He tells how it helped to tell his story and know that he isn't weird and that others had similar experiences (plate 1.7). When he is having a hard time he remembers all the things Helping Hannah taught him, especially when she told him he was very brave and a survivor (plate 1.8) and this helps him feel better.

Plate 1.3

Plate 1.4

Plate 1.5

Plate 1.6

Plate 1.7

Plate 1.8

Brave Bart is also used with parents whose children have been traumatized as well. Asking parents to read *Brave Bart* helps to educate them about trauma, normalize some of their fears, be informed about the intervention process and reduce anxiety by learning that children can learn to survive.

The same process is used with adolescents. Examples of what other adolescents experience, their thoughts, emotions, and behaviors help to normalize reactions. Stressing that a trauma is unlike any other experience helps adolescents understand the need for help. The range of reactions and thoughts are reviewed so the adolescent no longer feels strange and that the intervenor also has a good understanding of what trauma is like. Often the time taken to educate children and normalize their reactions before beginning intervention helps bring relief and a willingness to continue.

This Is Me - This is What Happened

The child is asked in the first session to draw a picture of what happened that he can then tell a story about. He is also asked to draw a picture of the person who was victimized. This begins the sensory intervention. Trauma-specific questions are directed at identifying details as well as what the experience was like.

Plate 2 was drawn by a three year old as she told the story of her mother and father hitting each other. She identified herself, mother and father as specific dots in the drawing. Her mother was hospitalized following this incident, and the child was terrified her mother was dying.

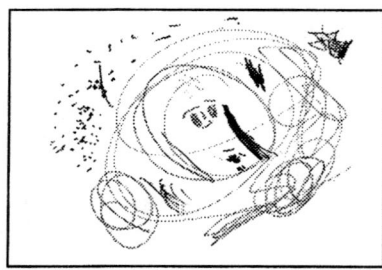

Plate 2

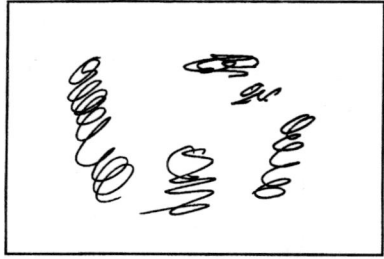

Plate 3

Plate 4

This is Me

Plate 3 was drawn by a six year old boy who was sexually abused by an uncle six months prior to intervention. This was his drawing for "This is Me". Keep in mind that drawing is not for the purpose of evaluation or analysis, but to engage the child at the sensory level. The drawing only represents what the child indicates it represents. During this task the child talked about his being a "bad boy" for doing a bad thing. This detail allowed the intervenor to approach his parents who had no idea that their son was feeling like a bad boy. He had never said this to them. This distorted, disconnected "self" drawing is an example of the way trauma can attack, distort and at times "disfigure" one's identity as well as define, for the victim, the way he views himself now, after the trauma.

Plate 4 is a self portrait (*This is Me*) of Sally, an eight year old girl. Her mother died one year earlier of cancer. Her mother spent the last six months of her life at home. Her daughter was exposed to a variety of very difficult scenes.

Plate 4.1 (*This is What Happened*) is her drawing of what happened to her mom. In this drawing her mom had not died yet. She was in a hospital bed with her cancer. Some children, when asked to draw a picture of what happened to the victim who died, will not initially draw the victim as dead. For some, the story of what happened before the death is as important as the death itself.

Because Sally did not draw a picture of her mom dead, she was then asked to draw a picture of what her mom looked dead. Plate 4.2 certainly makes us a witness to an entirely different part of her story.

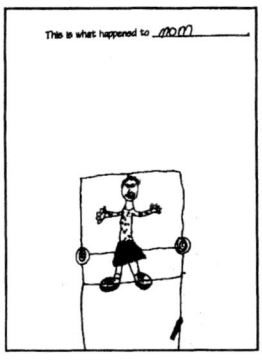
Plate 4.1

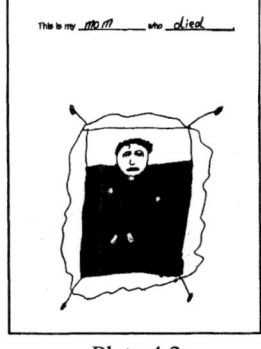
Plate 4.2

Sixteen year old James, was seen for disruptive behavior in school, declining grades and several other problems. There had been a significant, on-going trauma in this youngster's life. Although it was uncertain as to whether he was ever physically abused, his mother had a history of being abused by the men in her life. Five years earlier his mother was jailed for hiring a "hit man" to kill her husband. She was paroled, began visiting her son and three months later jailed once again for criminal behavior. This youngster's good friend was shot and killed a year earlier and his uncle drove his car into a telephone pole. Needless to say this youngster had some problems.

The activity, *"This is Me"* asks adolescents to circle those caricatures that best reflect themselves. They are given three pages of caricatures, in addition to a blank page to draw those caricatures that were not included in the worksheets. This is much easier than asking adolescents to draw a picture of themselves. Plate 5 is an example of what James circled. Following this task the adolescent is then asked to briefly describe what each caricatures is about.

Plate 5

This activity also allows the intervenor the opportunity to move the victim into survivor thinking. The teen is asked, "As you look at all that you circled, what comes to mind?" In most cases the response will be something like, "There are many parts to me." This is a foundation for survivor thinking and accomplishes reframing at a sensory level. Imagine saying to a teen, "What happened to you is unfortunate but there are many different parts to your life. Your trauma is only one part." At a cognitive level this will be interpreted as minimizing and being insensitive and unknowing. At a sensory level, after this activity, the teen experiences (knows) this before reframing it cognitively. The response now is one that is much easier to accept and helps the adolescent shift his focus to a survivor response.

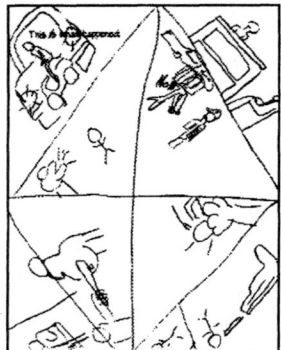

Plate 5.1

Plate 5.1 (*This is What Happened*) demonstrates the desire victims have to tell their story. It was not enough for James just to talk about his mom; he included the other traumas in his life.

When asked to draw a picture of his mother, Plate 5.2, the visual representation was quite different than expected, but became the focal point for him to talk about the trauma and conflict created by his mother.

Plate 5.2

Worry

van der kolk (1996) identified worry about the safety of a family member or friend following an incident as one of six factors involved in the complexity of a child's reaction to trauma. Schwarz and Kowalski (1991) also reported that worry about the safety of self and others was related to proximity of sixty-four children interviewed following a school shooting in an elementary school in suburban Chicago in 1988. The female adult perpetrator killed one child and wounded six other children before leaving the school and killing herself at a nearby home.

Questions about worry for the safety of loved ones, about the family of the deceased child and injured children, and about personal safety were asked. Eighty one percent of the children worried about someone during or following the event. The authors suggested that worry as an "emotional state" might be equivalent to proximity to the event and a variable in symptom formation. Longigan et al. (1991) also found this to be the case.

The SITCAP model identifies the nature and level of severity of the child's primary worry early in intervention. It returns at the end of intervention to determine the status of the child's worry. In field tests and research, the level of worry severity at the beginning intervention frequently corresponded to the overall level of severity of all reactions. Changes in worry at the conclusion of intervention also corresponded to changes in severity of reactions following intervention.

Although research is continuing, the evidence has been substantial enough for the Institute to give the child the opportunity to address the worry that may be driven by his trauma experience. This also is managed at the sensory level and then reframed cognitively as needed.

Plate 6 depicts the size (level) of Sally's worry, the eight year old girl whose mother died of cancer. The worry, one year later, was about her dog running away and dying. The only parent in the home was the father. Extended family had not been readily accessible. Her dog was her best friend. Children are instructed to fill in the box that best represents how small or big the worry is for them. Sally's worry was significant, as significant as the level of severity of her reactions across the three major sub-categories of the DSM-IV PTSD diagnostic criteria.

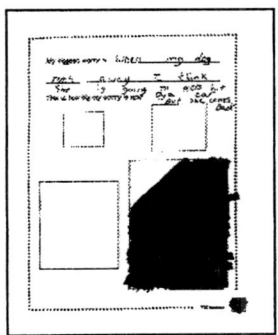

Plate 6

In the final session, worry was reviewed to determine if the level of severity had decreased. Plate 6.1 depicts an almost fifty percent reduction in Sally's worry, which corresponded to her overall reduction in scores on the PTSD Child Adolescent Questionnaire.

Plate 7 is a self portrait of Sam, age ten, whose mother killed herself when he was seven years old. Three years later his major worry, which had never been addressed, was that his mother was in hell (plate 7.1). The intensity of his worry at a sensory level was such that in making the intervenor a witness to how big a worry this was for him, he almost tore the paper. Worry is a sensation following trauma that is seldom addressed in the literature, yet is a major issue for victims.

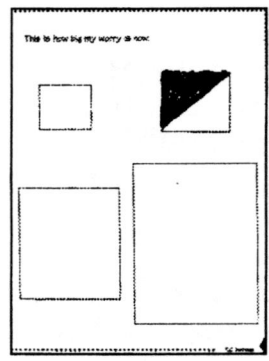

Plate 6.1

Plate 7

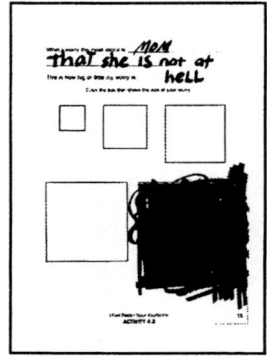

Plate 7.1

Hurt

Hurt following a trauma is frequently experienced physically, but often goes unattended, especially when the trauma did not involve any form of injury or physical assault to the child.

Plate 8 illustrates Sam's perception of where his mother felt the hurt the most and then where he felt the hurt the most. Sam's mother killed herself. Sam found her in the car when he came home from school.

In this case Sam had a number of visits to the school nurse for stomach aches throughout the year. These were never addressed from a trauma perspective until Sam himself was given the opportunity to not only talk about his hurt, but show the intervenor what that hurt looked like.

Plate 9 illustrates Sally's hurt (mom's cancer) and what it looked like. In this example she had the need to not only draw what her hurt looked like, but what hurt the most. She was actually ahead of the process by describing what it was that caused this terrible thing to happen to her mom. Her hurt was sad and mad.

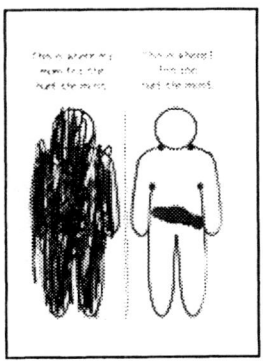

Plate 8

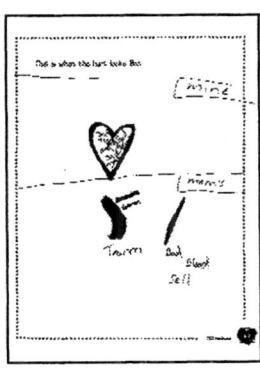

Plate 9

An eleven year old boy, we'll call Frank, had responded to his sister's murder one year earlier by becoming assaultive. When asked trauma-specific questions about "hurt", he was only asked to describe it, not draw it. Questions about where he felt it the most in his body, what made the hurt come back, what he would do when the hurt was there, and what would help the hurt go away, were all questions he was asked.

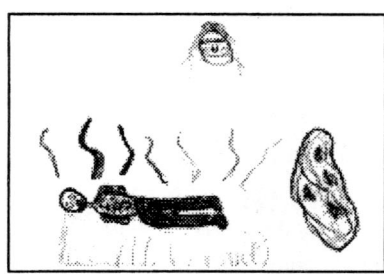

Plate 10

Approximately twenty minutes later, the intervenor was bringing the session to a close. Frank was reminded that if he were alone and having reactions he could draw those reactions. At this point he picked up his pencil and said to the intervenor, "Remember that hurt we were talking about? This is what that hurt looks like (Plate 10)." The hurt is represented in the form to the right of his sister's body. This is a critical demonstration of how important it is for a traumatized child to communicate at a sensory level and how drawing can communicate what words cannot describe. Once he made the intervenor a witness to his hurt, he put his pencil down and said, "Okay, now I'm done."

Anger, Revenge, Accountability

Sam, the boy whose mother killed herself, was an angry youngster. The anger (plate 11) had not been directed into assaultive behavior, but turned inward. He was also sad, but did not express that sadness until he was asked to draw his anger.

At the core of trauma-driven anger is a sense of powerlessness. His mother's suicide made no sense nor had he been able to make sense of it. The hurt he experienced in his stomach was also a "storage" place for his anger.

Plate 11

Focus is spent on coping and responding differently to trauma-driven anger. As a child who is helped to feel safer, he is able to re-experience a renewed sense of power and develop a different understanding (reframing) of his trauma, the anger is more likely to defuse itself. Helping Sam externalize that anger safely into his trauma container (8 1/2" x 11" sheet of paper) and giving him the opportunity to tell his story (give it a language) allowed him to reorder his whole experience in a way that was not only manageable, but brought him relief. Plate 11.1 is a drawing from the final session showing how he felt at the end of intervention.

Part of the process when dealing with anger and revenge is to have the child draw a picture of what he would like to see happen to the person or thing that caused this (his trauma) to happen. Sally first drew (Plate 12) the cancer that caused her mother's death.

Following the story she told about these cancer cells, she drew a picture (Plate 12.1) of what she wanted to see happen to them. The lines represented the cells that she then turned into bombs and vocally exploded each and every one of them.

Plate 11.1

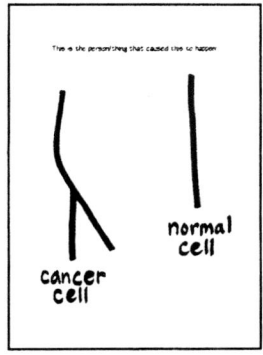

Plate 12

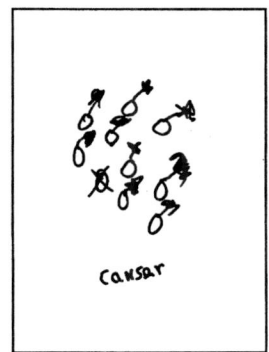

Plate 12.1

It is not the purpose of this intervention to treat deep rooted rage. If rage remains severe following this intervention process, additional long term treatment may be advisable. Certainly school settings, but even many clinical settings, are not designed to appropriately treat rage, a force that cannot be tamed by short term intervention. A combination of psychotherapy, behavioral interventions and medication may all be needed in some cases.

Following violent victimization, revenge is always a possibility. Preoccupation with getting even is not abnormal yet, if not dealt with, can lead to many problems including the intended pursuit of taking revenge. When weapons are accessible to children who have been victimized, the risk for the victim to become the perpetrator is high. This has certainly proven true in sexual and physical abuse cases when years have gone by without intervention or even knowledge of the abuse of the child. Any concern about the potential to actively pursue revenge is to be taken seriously and responded to accordingly. Anger is approached to identify the possible presence of revenge. In trauma, it is also viewed as the face of powerlessness. The focus on anger is also a natural introduction to the presence of guilt, also a face for powerlessness.

Accountability

Guilt is not an uncommon response to trauma. Survivor guilt has two levels; "It was my fault" and, "It should have been me instead." As in anger, at the core of guilt is the sense of powerlessness. In the aftermath of trauma, guilt, shame and powerless are often all experienced.

Besides addressing what the worst part of the experience was when addressing guilt, what the best thing the child did is also addressed to help keep him focused on his internal resources. Some education about flight, freeze and fright also bear repeating at this time. These are reactions that are often held secretly by victims who are ashamed about "not being able to move to reach in the overturned car and pull out their sister", to be able to "yell for help", or to have stopped themselves from running. It is important to normalize all these reactions and to educate the child to arousal and the mid-brain responses when faced with a life threatening, terrifying situation. It is important to educate victims to the fact that the mid brain "chooses" the immediate response to a trauma and that victims cannot generally make an immediate, purely cognitive choice in the initial few minutes. The mid brain triggers an automatic behavioral response.

Suicide

Prolonged living in the state of powerlessness induced by trauma can certainly lead to feelings of helplessness, haplessness and then hopelessness, the precedents of suicide. Guilt and shame only add to the pain and intensity of feeling hopeless. Although research related to the relationship between posttraumatic stress disorder and suicide in children is almost nonexistent, practitioners must remain sensitive to suicide as a final resolution of an unresolved trauma state. Adolescents in the SITCAP model are asked to give a numerical indication of how frequently they experience thoughts that are related to suicidal patterns. "Nothing ever changes.", " No matter what I do, it's always the same." are examples. Asking any victim about suicidal ideations and behaviors is critical.

Future Orientation

The DSM-IV (APA, 1994) identifies the absence of future orientation as a criteria of PTSD. Those who are unable to make the shift from relating to life as a victim versus a survivor have been unable to reconnect themselves to a future. Loss of future orientation is also related to suicide. Re-connecting the child to a future is paramount to healing.

The SITCAP model's focus on activities directed at first seeing oneself as a survivor and then engaging life as a survivor, is about rebuilding hope for the future and experiencing a renewed sense of power to "protect" oneself in the face of future trauma.

Although cognitive reframing is an important process, hope still must be "known" at the sensory level in order to trigger the energy to act on behalf of ones own life. *Brave Bart* goes a long way in helping children "know" hope. For adolescents an activity titled *Road Map to the Future* is used to help them with re-connecting to the future at a sensory level, then cognitive level.

James, the sixteen year old whose mother was jailed, gave all the indications of a teenager without hope, without connection to the future. To have his mother go to jail a second time after she had reinitiated visits with him was devastating. His drawing of a prison wall with bars in response to *This is My Mother* was a depersonalization of not only his mother, but of himself. The detachment, the numbing was among other reasons for referral. This was the type of youngster that, unfortunately, many attempted to help through approaching him cognitively. Asking this youngster to tell what was bothering him only created more resistance. His 'self' had been lost as had his hope. He needed to experience a 'sensory' reunion with his 'lost self' so as to 'sense' himself as a survivor in order to then renew hope and begin work on redirecting himself to the future.

Plate 13 illustrates the *Road Map to the Future* Worksheet that directs the teen to begin with his earliest memory and move to the present listing the "not so good" as well as good things that happened to him. The listing begins at the bottom and moves upward in sequence as a sensory way of experiencing "life in forward motion" and coming to "know" that despite what has happened, he is surviving. This "survivor thinking" is then later reinforced cognitively by the intervenor but more often by the child who begins to see his life differently as it is "mapped out" in front of him.

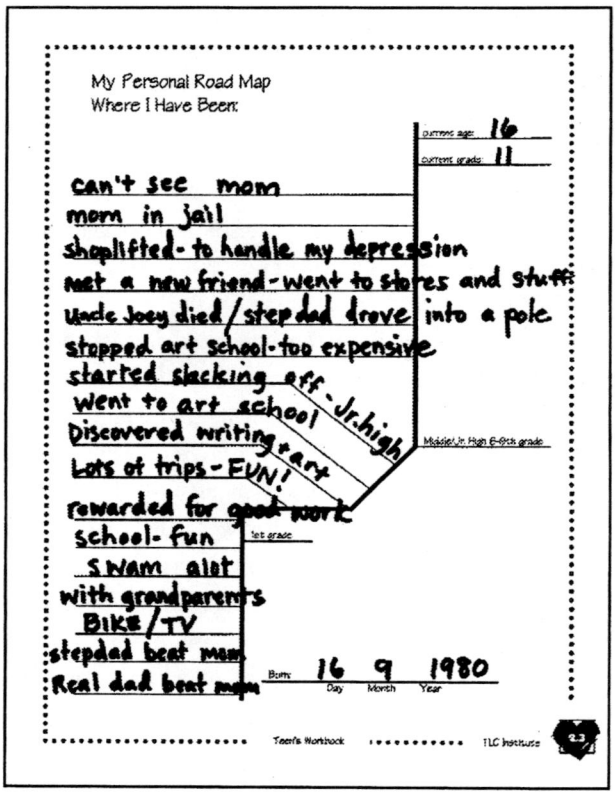

Plate 13

One of the purposes of having a structured, sequential focus on all the major themes of trauma is because we cannot know how to be the most helpful. Some children do not have major issues with hurt, while for others the theme of hurt holds or becomes the reference point for the most severest, the most intense reactions. By approaching each theme we give the child the opportunity to find and safely expose himself to the most difficult part of his experience while at the same time surviving that exposure. The *Road Map to the Future* became an empowering experience for Jeff.

Jeff was asked to just sit and look at his road map for a minute and then he was asked, "As you look at your road map what one thought stands out most in your mind?" His response was, "I'm still here, that must mean something." The response by the intervenor was, "It means you are a survivor."

The road map also became a tool to identify those happy times, good times and safe places to return. At the sensory level, these experiences became resources to strengthen and define his positive self. In Jeff's travels he made the intervenor a witness to the fact that he was supported by others in his life, that he was able to enjoy himself, that he did have a dream (to be an artist or writer). All of these became a part of reframing his view of himself that, until this intervention, had previously been one of himself and as a victim. At the same time this "visual road map" gave the intervenor a different look at Jeff that a cognitive approach would not have revealed.

Trauma-specific Questions

Very specific questions are directed to the major themes of trauma and designed to help the child tell his story. These questions ask about details of the incident, but also about the reactions to that incident. They are not leading or open ended, nor do they ask for feelings.

The following examples are not inclusive. They do not address all the major themes, survivor issues, and coping patterns. As these questions are an integral part of the exposure and trauma narrative process, results will be more beneficial when used as part of the intervention process and activities related to these questions, which is demonstrated in several ways during the Institute's training.

Draw me a picture you can tell me a story about...
Who are the people in your drawing?
What are each of them doing?
When this first happened or when you first found out, what do you remember doing?
What do you remember seeing - touching - smelling - hearing?
If the people (pets, etc.) in your drawing could talk what would they say?
Is there anyone or anything not in your drawing that needs to be there?
Where are you?
As you look at your drawing what jumps out (stands out) most to you now?
(Questions asked about every detail of the drawing.)

I want you to draw me a picture of the person who died (was killed, critically injured, taken from you, etc.) [*The worksheets include various directions to correspond with the specific incident, divorce, foster placement, physical abuse.*]

What can you tell me about ____?
What do you think ____ was thinking when this happened?
What was the worst part of what happened then?
What is the worst part now as you think about it?
What scared you the most then?
What scares you the most now?
As you think about it now, what surprised you the most about how you acted, what you thought?
When this happened did you freeze (unable to move or scream)?
When this first happened where do you remember feeling the hurt/fear the most in your body?

Draw me a picture of what that fear/hurt looks like?
If your hurt/fear had a name what would it be?
If your hurt/fear could talk what would it say?
If it could listen what would you say to it?

Case examples detailed earlier support the value of these very specific questions. They are also designed to keep the intervenor in the role of "witness". Chapter Ten will answer specific process questions. The SITCAP intervention process itself can only be "known" at a sensory level. This chapter presented a framework of the focused sequence and typical activities used, but it is a "cognitive" presentation that for some may not seem "therapeutic". The healing is in the "sensory living" of this intervention that itself cannot be adequately described by words alone. The authors again encourage training as a way to experience its value at a sensory level, to "know" as the children and their parents come to "know" it.

CHAPTER EIGHT

Parent Model
Session One

SITCAP Parent Model Overview

Help is also provided for those parents whose children have been traumatized. In addition to helping these parents with their own personal reactions, assistance is given them to help respond to the needs of their traumatized children.

Each of the eight sessions in this model will be briefly reviewed with the intent of identifying the primary strategies and objectives of these sessions. Not all parents will need eight sessions. The SITCAP model is also designed to provide brief intervention. At times one or two sessions is all that is needed. Not all activities will be examined, as that would necessitate a book of it's own. The process that is applied to the interventions for children and adolescents is applied to parent interventions. Exposure, trauma narrative and cognitive reframing remain the primary intervention strategies. A case example is presented in the final segment of this chapter.

Session one involves six activities: structuring the process, normalizing the trauma, debriefing, obtaining trauma history, assessment of reactions, and preparation for the next session.

The objectives include being able to:
- Provide the parents with the tools and resource materials needed to accelerate healing from trauma-inducing incidents;
- Prevent, if initiated within four to six weeks following the trauma, the development of posttraumatic stress disorder;
- Help parents continue and or return to pre-trauma parental functions and responsibilities;
- Help prevent the parent's traumatic experience from inducing anxiety and problematic behavior in their children.

Structuring Statements

Imagine yourself as a parent in crisis, feeling confused, overwhelmed, and fearful of losing control. It has been suggested that you seek help. You have never had counseling before, but you agree to an appointment. That decision has now presented you with an entirely new set of unknowns that further intensify your anxiety. When you walk through that counselor's door and first sit down, what is going to be the most helpful, most comforting introduction that the counselor can provide? Will it be a brief greeting and then the question, "So tell me what brings you here?" No, this does not lower anxiety.

In a crisis state what we need is structured information so that we can feel somewhat prepared for what we are about to do or for what is about to be done to us. By structuring the intervention process, you can reduce the parent's anxiety and also establish yourself as a sensitive intervenor who respects their right to know what they are about to "receive" from you. It helps return a level of control to the parent. It can remove many of the unknowns and myths that parents generally have about counselors and therapists, and allow them to begin to focus on and even anticipate an early resolution. With anxiety levels reduced, a parent can focus her energies on resolving the crisis.

Structuring statements are initiated after introductions. Following are several of the recommended statements for use when the child has also been traumatized.
- I understand you are here because _____. We will return to this situation, but first I want to talk to you briefly about the intervention process. It is important for you to know how this works.

- Today I will discuss with you what we mean by trauma and how trauma reactions are really different from other grief reactions you may be having.
- I will be asking you many questions about how your child was before and after the trauma so we can better evaluate what approaches would best benefit you and your child.
- Intervention will consist of a minimum of two, but no more than eight sessions, unless there is agreement that you would like to continue with issues still needing attention.
- I think we can say that participation is likely to ease tension in your personal and family relationships.
- You will, because of what you learn, be better able to cope with what has happened.
- Should you agree to continue, we would anticipate two outcomes:
  - The problem is resolved, or
  - The problem is not resolved, but we will be better able to identify what and perhaps who else is needed to resolve it. At the same time, we believe even if it is not resolved, you and your child will feel less frightened by what is happening. Certainly you will be more knowledgeable and very likely to feel more in control so the situation will not be as threatening, as difficult to manage or as disruptive to your everyday life...

Why This Approach is Encouraged

It has been our experience that counselors and helping professionals in general find this process difficult to implement. This is partially due to training that tends to ignore or shy away from such a direct approach. It is also partially due to the helper's anxiety that discussing such issues before moving into the problem areas, given the emotional state of the client, is often too much for family members in crisis to manage. The fact is that this structuring helps them to better manage their emotions, and so we strongly encourage its practice as a valid intervention strategy.

This kind of structuring may seem like more than enough, but family members really appreciate and respect the information and preparation. Rarely are those in crisis told what is about to happen by intervenors, whether they be counselors or physicians. Nor are clients usually "empowered" by counselors as to their participation in the counseling process, or communicated to with such directness about the expected length of counseling, the possible outcomes, their role as it relates to interactions with the intervenor, or the reassurance available should the process not work as planned. For these reasons we again strongly encourage the use of this structuring process.

Normalizing the Trauma

This is the initiation of a brief education of the differences between grief and trauma, the specific reactions of trauma and what is needed to help find relief from the terror of the experience. SITCAP provides a booklet titled, *What Parents Need to Know*, to assist with this education process. This process is designed to help reduce anxiety while encouraging intervention. This book begins with examples of incidents that can cause a personal trauma (this is not an inclusive listing):

- You witness a car accident that kills two people;
- A family member dies suddenly;
- Your parent dies after suffering from a terminal illness;
- You're robbed at gun point;
- You are physically or sexually assaulted;
- You are in a car accident that leaves you shaken or critically injured;
- You are diagnosed with a serious illness;
- A family member commits suicide;
- A family member is murdered;
- Divorce papers are filed.

The information presented over the next several pages is the information given to parents.

When a Trauma Occurs You Will Need Help

No matter how emotionally stable we are, a traumatic incident can present us with reactions we never have had to deal with previously. No matter how emotionally stable we are, a traumatic experience can leave us feeling vulnerable, powerless and out of control. No matter how emotionally stable we are, a traumatic experience can throw us off balance, make us doubt ourselves, create confusion, leave us anxious and uncertain, make it difficult to concentrate and remember, difficult to sleep, relax and relate to others, even those who are closest to us.

In the first four weeks following a trauma expect any of these reactions to be triggered (Examples are given for each):

- Recurrent, intrusive, distressing recollections of the event, including images, thoughts, or perceptions;
- Recurrent, distressing dreams of the event;
- Acting or feeling as if the traumatic event were recurring (includes a sense of reliving the experience, illusions, hallucinations, and dissociative flashback episodes, including those that occur upon awakening or when intoxicated);
- Intense psychological distress at exposure to internal cues that symbolize or resemble an aspect of the traumatic event (fear, anxiety, anger are possible examples);
- Physiological reactivity upon exposure to internal or external cues that symbolize or resemble an aspect of the traumatic event (nausea, difficulty breathing, faintness are a few examples);
- Trying to avoid thoughts, feelings, or conversations associated with the trauma;
- Trying to avoid activities, places, or people that arouse recollections of the trauma;
- Inability to recall an important aspect of the trauma;
- Diminished interest or participation in significant activities;
- Feeling of detachment or estrangement from others;
- Restricted range of affect (e.g., unable to have loving feelings);

- Sense of a foreshortened future (e.g., does not expect to have a career, marriage, or children, or a normal life span);
- Difficulty falling or staying asleep;
- Irritability or outbursts of anger;
- Difficulty concentrating;
- Hypervigilance - chronic state of fear/intense worry that something else is about to happen, constant state of alert;
- Exaggerated startle response (jumpy, easily startled).

These reactions are not at all unusual during the first four weeks following a traumatic event. Reactions may extend beyond the four week period when a person is involved in disasters or other external events, where physical reminders cannot be avoided. The same may occur when the details of an incident are kept alive in the media for an extended period of time.

If any of these reactions continue four weeks beyond the period from when the trauma happened, help is needed by most. Help is needed only because what is being experienced is new and unfamiliar. How we negotiate other problems is not the same way we negotiate trauma.

What Kind of Help is Needed?

The kind of help you need is called debriefing and reframing. Debriefing and reframing are ways to overcome your trauma. Debriefing involves answering specific questions about your experience that in most cases no one has ever asked. It involves telling your story in a way you probably have not been given an opportunity to do at other times. It involves making the Trauma Specialist a "witness" to your experience through your drawings. It includes telling the Trauma Specialist about the reactions you may be having, reactions that are common to most trauma - the fear, the worry, the hurt, the anger, the revenge, the guilt.

Reframing involves understanding the ways you have been victimized by your traumatic experience. Reframing involves discovering how your trauma reactions keep you a victim, and how to change your thinking from that of a "victim" to that of a "survivor".

Drawing

Drawing is a way to make us a witness to your experience. Drawing also helps you find relief from your trauma.

Drawing is:
- A safe way to find relief from the terror of your experience.
- An opportunity to tell of your experience in ways we often do not have words to describe.
- An opportunity to regain a sense of power over your experience.
- An opportunity to remember details that help make sense of what happened.
- An opportunity to now see your experience differently, in a way you can now better manage.

It doesn't matter what you draw or how you draw. When parents tell their stories they use stick figures, circles and squares. Drawing and the questions your Trauma Specialist or Consultant will be asking become a way to take the terror out of your trauma.

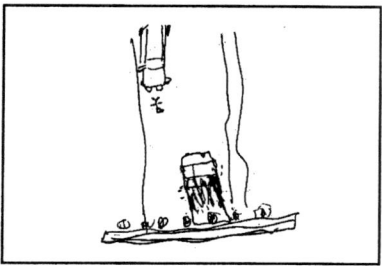

Plate 10.1

Examples of Adult Drawings

Plate 10.1 is the drawing by a 35 year old mother. An eighteen wheeler lost control, and jumped the medium. She hit the truck, went under it and was left for dead.

Plate 10.2

Plate 10.2 is a drawing of an angry person by a 42 year old mother.

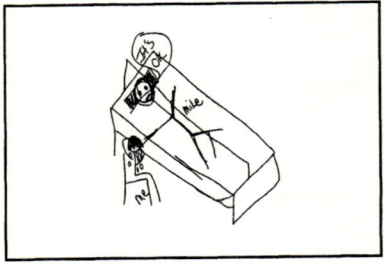

Plate 10.3

Plate 10.3 is a drawing by a 42 year old daughter whose father killed himself. Her father had called her to see if she needed him to visit with her family. She said "no", and felt for a long time that if she had said "yes", he'd still be alive.

Instructions for the Intervenor

Trauma History

The history taken is specific to the trauma and its variables. Variables include whether the parent was a victim, witness, or related to the victim, intervention provided, if any, medication usage, current major worries of the parent related to the trauma, and any major problems prior to the trauma. This brief history readies the parent to focus on details generated by debriefing.

Debriefing

The purpose of debriefing is to accelerate the healing process. Questions will vary according to whether the parent was a victim, witness, or neither victim nor witness, but related to the victim. Some examples follow.

If the parent was the victim or the witness ask:
- _____ tell me just briefly what happened?
- When this happened, and as you think about it now, what do you remember seeing?
- What do remember hearing?
- Are there any sounds that remind you of what happened?
- Are there any smells?
- Any sensations of touch?
- What do you remember doing?
- What is the first thing that happened?

Make sure the parent answers the question asked. Keep them focused. If they wander off into feelings, repeat the question and let the parent know she will have an opportunity to talk about feelings later.

If not a victim or witness but related to the victim (spouse, close friend, co-worker, etc.) ask:
- When you first found out what do you remember doing?
- Afterward, was there anything you saw that still stands out that you still see in your head?
- Does anything else remind you of what happened - color, sounds, smells?

The remaining questions can be asked of the victim, witness or those related to the victim.
- Of all that happened what was the worst part for you?
- What about that made it the worst part?
- Was there anything you wish you hadn't done?
- As you think about it now, what scared you the most then?
- What scares you the most now?
- When this happened what was your biggest worry?
- What is your biggest worry now?
- What do you think would cause this person to do this (if there was a perpetrator) or, if this is due to illness, car accident, etc. why do you think this happened?

Debriefing begins at the cognitive level. It is a safe place for the parent to begin. It allows for a slow, safe and structured return to the emotional reactions associated with the traumatic experience. This in not a time to be reflective, interpretive or analytical. Listen to the answer for each question and then move to the next question. You can normalize what you are told when finished. To do more than listen prohibits the parent from telling their story and making some "sense" of what happened.

Trauma Assessment

Assessment is completed following the debriefing process. The assessment is designed to identify the specific reactions present, the level of severity, the sub-category the reactions belong to (reexperiencing, avoidance, arousal), and the level of overall severity of each of the three sub-categories. Assessment is important as it provides a baseline to later compare with the final assessment to determine outcome and, when appropriate, substantiate the need for additional intervention.

Preparation for the Next Session

This preparation includes informing the parent of the following information:
- I want to reiterate that what you experienced was very traumatic. The reactions you are having, which are mostly new for you, are not at all unusual following such a situation. Your reactions and what you are experiencing are very normal.
- What we did today may trigger some additional memories. If you are unsure whether your memories are accurate, call someone who might be able to verify them. If there is no one to verify them, know that even though the details may not be accurate, the reactions associated with them are likely to be real and part of your sensory memory of the experience.
- Do not be alarmed by any new reactions. If new reactions emerge, it usually is an indication that you are feeling safe enough and strong enough to now deal with them.
- The fact is, you have survived. You have not given in to that terrifying experience. Otherwise you would not be here.
- I know this is not at all easy. It can be frightening to "go back". But in going back you can find strength and relief. Revisiting the experience can help to make sense of what happened. It provides the opportunity to see things differently and reorder what happened in a way that is now manageable.
- Next session we will review your evaluation, answer any questions you have, revisit some of what happened, and learn ways to help you find relief. Certainly if you need to call me before we meet, here is my number.

- Between now and our next session there are some things I want you to do to take care of yourself.

A few of the following suggestions directly refer to the first several weeks following exposure. If the parent's trauma was several months earlier and she is just now seeking help, eliminate the wording "4-6 weeks" and substitute "during intervention".

Helpful Ways to Care for Yourself

- It is very important to your recovery to get enough rest, especially the first 4 to 6 weeks following the trauma.
    - If you cannot sleep at night, take "cat" naps of 15 minutes - 1/2 hour during the day.
    - If you wake up during the night because of traumatic dreams, know they will pass in time. Do what comforts you. Read a good book until you become sleepy again. Snack, watch television, listen to music, write, do some housework. Remember, this will be a temporary change.
- Exercise of some kind is important to help relieve you of the tension that traumatic experiences create. Even if you have not been exercising, go for a short walk. Walk the dog an extra time. Do housework or add a few minutes to your usual exercise routine.
- Pull back on making a commitment to additional responsibilities for the first four weeks. The tendency for some is to take on additional responsibilities thinking it will help them forget. In reality, it frequently drains them of energy, delays the healing process, and intensifies future reactions when they finally emerge.
- Be protective and nurturing of yourself. It's okay to want to be by yourself, or just stay around home with the family. Eat whatever your comfort foods are, as frequently as you need. Do those things which relax you, give you some pleasure.

Following this activity the parent is told that in the next session the assessment results will be reviewed and that they will begin work on getting some relief.

Session Two

There are eight activities in the second session: educating and normalizing, exposure (making us a witness), attending to details (telling the story), sensory relief, hurt and fear, anger and worry, recapitulation, becoming a survivor.

The objectives of this session are:
- To review and normalize outcome of assessment;
- To address the major themes of fear, terror, worry, hurt, anger, revenge, accountability, safety, powerlessness, and survivor versus victim thinking;
- To identify which of the above are creating the most intense reactions;
- To help the parent experience at a sensory level some relief and, at the same time, a renewed sense of power over their experience;
- To begin cognitively reframing the experience to move the parent from "victim thinking" to "survivor thinking".

Educating and Normalizing

A review of the outcome of the assessment is initiated followed by definition of the specific reactions identified and the normalizing of these reactions. Further education about trauma and attention to normalizing is continued with the support of the booklet, *What Parents Need to Know*. This segment discusses and illustrates how other parents were helped. It discusses secondary victimization, healing benchmarks, and an introduction to what is meant by the term "survivor". The overall intent of this process is to encourage the parents informed consent to continue with intervention.

Exposure (Making Us a Witness)

This is the exposure component of SITCAP which involves the use of drawing and trauma-specific questions related to the themes/sensations of trauma. It's function is to give the parent an opportunity to make us a witness to how she was impacted by her trauma by giving us a visual reference as to how she now views herself and the world around her as a result of her exposure.

This is a more intense involvement than the initial debriefing process in Session One. Sensory reactions similar to those experienced during the trauma will emerge but now allow the parent the opportunity to experience, at the sensory level, relief from and a renewed sense of power over these trauma sensations.

Because of the intensity of this experience it is important to inform the parent of the following:

- The first 10-15 minutes will probably be the most difficult for you emotionally, but also the most beneficial. At the end of this time I will help relieve you of those intense reactions. Many report remembering details they had forgotten, being able to make sense of things that didn't make sense before, and generally finding relief.
- Trauma is very universal. This means regardless of age, gender or ethnicity, reactions are quite common. Your reactions are quite normal given what you experienced. I think this is important for you to know. It is also important for you to know that you do not have to tell me anything about your reactions. You certainly can, but it is okay not to if it makes you uncomfortable. When we have finished, I'll be able to give you suggestions about ways to take care of yourself.

The initial activity of exposure focuses the parent on their traumatic experience followed by the drawing of a picture about the incident, which becomes the focal point for her to tell her story. The parent is assisted with the initial focusing through these directions:

- What I want you to do for a minute is to quietly begin to think about your experience - go ahead (pause);
- Now begin to see where this happened, all the objects in the environment - (pause). Begin to see the other people or things involved;
- Begin to hear what others are saying or any sounds that remind you of what happened - (pause). Recall any smells or sensations of touch like heat or cold that remind you of what happened;
- Let yourself recall the different parts of your experience. When you are ready, draw a picture of that experience that you can tell me a story about (pause). Stick figures are fine. It doesn't matter what you draw, or how well you draw, just that you draw.

Allow whatever time it takes for her to complete her drawing. If the parent is unsure how to start, let her know it doesn't matter where, anywhere is fine. If this doesn't help - ask what part of the story she is seeing or thinking about. Then just have her draw a line or circle. The line can be any part of the environment. The circle could be the face of the victim, herself or any other person in the story.

Once the parent completes her drawing, a series of questions are asked to help her tell her story. These questions initially attend to details (this is not an all inclusive listing of questions):

- Who are the people in your drawing and what is your relationship to them?
- When this first happened (or when you first found out), what do you remember doing?
- As you think about it now, what was your first thought when this happened?

The parent is directed to identify where in her body the experience is being felt the most. This helps in identifying the sensory memories. It also provides the opportunity to support the parent and to let her know that in a few minutes she will be given help to find sensory relief from the intensity of these reactions.

Attending to Details

A second drawing is requested of the person (victim) who was killed, died, left, was critically injured, etc. If the parent is the victim, ask her to draw a picture of herself at the time of victimization. Following this drawing, additional questions help add to the details of the story.

A psychomotor activity is initiated to further trigger memories of the experience. (The authors do not recommend initiating this activity without training.) The parent is asked to choose a part of the drawing (victim) she is going to trace for a two minute period. During tracing she is instructed to just let herself recall whatever comes to mind. This psychomotor activity can intensify feelings and sensory memories. It can create a level of safety through repetition. It can help the parent find relief from earlier reactions. It varies from parent to parent. The activity is again followed by very focused questions that begin to deal with the emotional memories without asking about feelings:

- As you look at your drawing, can you tell me what the worst part of that experience was for you then?
- As you think about it, what is the worst part for you now, if there is a worst part?
- What did you experience (not think about) while you were tracing?
- Now I want you to again pay attention to your body. (Pause) Tell me where you are experiencing this the most right now.

Sensory Relief

It is always important to create a balance between the intensity of trauma memories and the relief from those memories. Sensory relief allows for the developing of a sense of safety.

Finding Relief

Following are instructions to the parent for finding relief.
- Take a piece of paper and draw a sad line or what a sad line might look like.
- Now take some time, on the back of the paper draw a happy line.
- Now, think about the funest, happiest, most pleasurable time you can remember.
- <u>See it</u> happening all over again, <u>see the environment</u> - the different <u>objects, shapes, colors - see the people</u>, if any, that were part of this.
- Remember the sounds associated with this funest, happiest, most pleasurable time.
- Remember any specific sensation of touch, any smells.
- Now, as you are reliving this experience, I want you to use your happy line to draw a picture about your experience that you can tell me a story about.

After drawing ask:
- Who are the other people in your drawing? What are they doing, thinking, etc?
- Of this experience what was the funest, happiest, most pleasurable part?

- Tell me what about this made it the funest, happiest, most pleasurable part? (Do ask this question: It narrows the focus and allows for a more intense pleasant sensory experience which in turn helps to relieve the previous intense, sensory trauma reaction.)
- Where in your body are you experiencing this funest, happiest, most pleasurable experience?
- Now, tell me what has happened to the trauma part? (Common responses - "It's gone." "It's not as bad. It's moved.")

Cognitive Reframing

It is critical to present these responses:
- In the future you can control unwanted reactions by returning to a safe place in the way you did today.
- Memories of your trauma experience will never go away, but now you know you can replace those memories with positive memories and find relief.

When the parent's answer is - "Nothing has changed." or "It's still there." the intervenor's response is one that normalizes and supports the experience.
- You just learned that in the midst of your trauma you can also experience some pleasure and have pleasant memories. In time, as you are able to focus more on the pleasurable, pleasant times and all the different parts of your life, those trauma reactions will diminish. It also is very possible that as we go through the remaining activities in this program you will experience relief more than you do now.

If there is not expressed relief at the end of this session, it is likely that additional sessions will be needed. The session ends with an activity designed to focus on the "survivor part" of the parent.

As A Survivor

The following statements are presented:
- Like a wound that heals, the scar or memory will remain forever, but the pain will subside.

What is important to understand is:
- This is an ongoing process. It doesn't happen immediately;
- The way you think does drive how you behave, just as emotions like fear, drive how you react. There is a time in life when you simply must commit yourself to thinking differently about your situation. This is one of those critical times;
- To change the way you think and ultimately act, you must consciously work at repeating these survivors thoughts;
- We are not minimizing the pain of your experience. The memory of what happened will always be there. What we are doing is diminishing the hold that the experience has on you. (Reframing) You have been wounded deeply. It will take time to heal. When you heal there will be a scar. In this case, the memory, but the wound will no longer hurt at the level that it distracts you, or worries you, or scares you. Your scar or memory will in time remind you that you are a survivor, but also, that there are other parts of your life now that hold your attention and are important.

Hurt, Fear, Anger and Worry

These major themes of trauma are approached with the same process - drawing and trauma structured questions. The parent is asked to draw, for example, what the hurt/fear following her exposure looks like. Trauma questions then encourage the telling of the range of details and issues related to hurt or fear. With anger, the issue of revenge and guilt becomes the focus. Worry, which is a common trauma theme, identifies the primary focal point of the parent's worry.

The purpose of these activities is simply to help the parent identify the primary issue of each of these trauma themes. Subsequent sessions focus on activities to help the parent resolve those parts which are unwanted. Not every parent has an issue with revenge. For some, worry is the primary reaction keeping the trauma alive or the parent spending high levels of energy in trying to avoid the anxiety associated with her worry.

Recapitulation

This final activity is designed to help the parent complete the story, experience some closure, reinforce sensory relief. It's an opportunity to add details but also reinforce the fact that although reliving the experience was difficult some relief was also experienced. It is also not unusual for parents to reframe, in a positive way, her view of herself and the way her experience impacted her life.

The following questions and statements help structure this activity:
- As you look at all of the drawings what stands out the most for you?
- As you look at your drawings what surprises you the most?
- As you look at all of your drawings is there anyone or anything you need to add? Go ahead and make the addition. (Ask about what was added.)
- Which drawing helped you the most?
- As you think about this now, how did this change your view of life?

Summary Statements (made to parents)

- It is important to understand that as we went through this activity you did experience tension, but you also experienced some relief.
- That relief will increase in time, and I'll teach you ways to strengthen that relief.
- Although it may not seem like it now, you probably will think about your experience differently and not be so frightened by it. Over the next several sessions you'll regain more and more control over these reactions. Rather than continuing to be a victim of your experience, you will become a survivor.

Becoming a Survivor

Numerous activities are used in the final minutes to introduce the parent to the meaning of being a survivor. Following is a portion of the material used to identify survivor issues:

As A Survivor

We can now help you move from victim thinking to survivor thinking. As a survivor you will overcome your victimization with the help of your Trauma Specialist or Consultant.

As A Survivor:
- You will have a reduction in the number of times you experience trauma reactions;
- You will have less fear of these reactions;
- You will have less fear of losing control;
- You will have a renewed sense of hope and direction in your life;
- You will redevelop a sense of humor and experience more pleasure in life;
- You will have a profound understanding of other's pain;
- You will reestablish a positive relationship with your family;
- You will feel stronger because of what happened and develop a new, often profound view of life.

With the Help of Trauma-specific Intervention Your Thinking Will Change

As a survivor you will know and believe the following about yourself:

- ☐ Yes, bad situations come up in my life, but I can do things to make them better;
- ☐ I expect a lot of good to happen in my life;
- ☐ I am loveable and people love me;
- ☐ I may feel sad, angry, depressed and confused today, but I will not always feel this way. Things will get better;
- ☐ I have a lot to offer the world and I am motivated to go forward;

- ☐ I am capable. I handle life with confidence;
- ☐ I can trust most people;
- ☐ I am a worthy person. I have many traits that are worthwhile;
- ☐ I am only responsible for myself. I cannot control everything;
- ☐ Those who can will like me and understand me without a lot of explaining or apologizing;
- ☐ Everyone makes mistakes; that is how we learn;
- ☐ It is okay to be wrong. I am still a good person;
- ☐ People see me in a positive way;
- ☐ I take each day as it comes;
- ☐ I look forward to the future;
- ☐ I am in control of my life. There are things I can do to make my life better;
- ☐ My life is balanced;
- ☐ People are supportive of me. I trust my inner self to make good choices about others;
- ☐ I am strong. I face difficult situations head on;
- ☐ Each day I get a little stronger. I will get over this;
- ☐ I am a survivor. I need not apologize. I am surviving;
- ☐ As a survivor, I have many choices in my life.

Once again it is important to understand that it takes time to be a survivor. Being here is the beginning.

Session Three

This session devotes itself to the issues of secondary victimization (wounding) and a continuation of the developing of the survivor response. It has four activities: defining secondary victimization, identifying the presence of secondary victimization with the parent, the victim thinking patterns of the parent, and the many parts of the survivor self.

The objectives of Session Three are:
- To help the parent identify the ways trauma has been kept alive through secondary victimization;
- To help the parent develop and or strengthen the "survivor" response.

Defining Secondary Victimization

The following information is provided the parent:
- What often happens after exposure to a trauma is what is referred to as secondary victimization. This can prevent your recovery.
- Secondary victimization is when the people and organizations you turn to for help respond in ways, often quite subtle, that cause you additional pain or cause you to begin to blame yourself for what happened.
- The people and organizations you turn to for help are people you believe understand and can be helpful. You trust them. Because of your trust you tend to believe all, or part of what they tell you, even when their responses hurt and blame you.
- Secondary victimization leads to self-blame and guilt, which weakens your self image and prevents you from recovering and healing.

Parents are also provided handout material identifying the different types of "wounding". Material adapted from this prepares the parent to then identify secondary wounding experiences. The forms of secondary wounding include (presented to the parent):

- **Denial and disbelief**

When people tell you that you are exaggerating, that what you say happened couldn't have happened, that you were thrown off balance and didn't really remember, that your imagination was running wild are indicators that they do not believe or deny the reality of what is happening to you. Children who attempt to tell a parent about abuse by a spouse or another family member often meet with denial "Your uncle is a nice person..."

- **Discounting - minimizing**

When people tell you, "I have had to deal with people who have had it a lot harder than you." "You still have a whole future ahead of you." "Look, you're overreacting. I can tell you stories that are really terrible." "You shouldn't be upset. What happened, happened." "At least this only happened to you once."

"At least this is the only one terrible thing that has happened. There are a lot of others who are not so fortunate." are all ways of making you feel that you do not have a right to the terror and pain this incident has caused you. It is a way (wounding) of saying there is something wrong with you for letting this get control of you.

- **Blaming you**

When people tell you, "Well maybe if you hadn't..." "You should have never..." "That's what you get for..." "Well maybe if you had..." are the beginnings of statements that are accusatory and blaming. They are based on the belief that you are perfect and should never make mistakes or that you should be in control of everyone and everything around you.

- **Treating you as defective**

Following trauma some are quick to view you as emotionally flawed for life and communicate this in a variety of ways. Ridicule, labeling you as disturbed, weak, just wanting attention and sympathy, treating you as if you are now incompetent, undesirable somehow not a healthy person to be around. Some are outright cruel in calling you incompetent, stupid, and immature for letting this happen to you in the first place.

- **System victimization**

Although more attention and support is being provided victims through the Office of Victim's Assistance, some personnel in agencies, medical facilities, judicial systems, law enforcement and other settings still have the prevalent notion that " You get what you deserve in life and deserve what you get." Obviously this will hurt you deeply.

Many helping professionals are also suffering from what can seem like an impossible, unending line of people needing their services. Overworked and often under paid, they shut down, burn out and become emotionally unable to be helpful to those seeking help.

Identifying Secondary Victimization

At this time the parent needs help to identify the ways she may have been wounded. A checklist is used. Following are examples of statements on the checklist:

Secondary Victimization Checklist

____ You are exaggerating (about what happened).
____ It couldn't have happened that way.
____ You really can't remember that kind of detail.
____ Your imagination is running away with you.
____ He/she would never do that.
____ There are people who have had it harder than you.
____ Consider yourself lucky.
____ You're still young.
____ You're overreacting. You need to put this in perspective.

This checklist is not inclusive. It helps the parent to identify the ways she's been wounded. The process also serves to acknowledge what, in most cases, has never been acknowledged. Without acknowledgement, wounding can keep the parent trapped by additional victimization that only victims understand.

Victim Identification

Once wounded, the "victim response" to life often intensifies. The thoughts associated with relating to ones experience as a victim can lead to additional victimization. At the core of being stuck in "victim thinking" is powerlessness and hopelessness. Depression often follows. In order to move into a survivor response the parent must first identify the victim thinking patterns that can prevent movement to becoming a survivor and reclaiming her life. On the following page are some examples of victim thinking.

130

Victim Thinking

Following is a partial list of statements reflective of individuals who think and behave as victims. (Matsakis, *Aphrodite: Post-Traumatic Stress Disorder*, New Harbinger Publications, Inc., CA. 1994)

To begin, check the **boxes** beside those statements that sound like something you find yourself thinking or feeling.

- ☐ I have to accept bad situations because they are part of life and I can do nothing to make them better.
- ☐ I don't expect much good to happen in my life.
- ☐ Nobody could ever love me.
- ☐ I am always going to feel sad, angry, depressed, and confused.
- ☐ There are situations at work and at home that I could do something about, but I don't have the motivation to do so.
- ☐ Life overwhelms me, so I prefer to be alone whenever possible.
- ☐ You can't trust anyone except a few people.
- ☐ I feel I have to be extra good, competent, and attractive in order to compensate for my many defects.

The Many Parts of Becoming a Survivor

This activity is critical to movement into viewing self as a survivor. At a sensory level it is a safe activity, one that is fun as well. It helps with expanding sensory relief as well as strengthening the cognitive reframing of the parent's view of self.

This activity involves circling the symbols which cover their worksheets. The symbols are reflective of the many different parts that make up our personality and identity. The circling process is a continuation of the drawing (psychomotor) activity which keeps the parent at a sensory level.

Following are a few examples of the symbols:

The activity is introduced with the following statements:
- You have done a lot of work today. I want to again stress that the reactions you are having are not at all unusual. They are quite normal. As a survivor we can help you find relief from the terror of your experience. The fact is, you have already moved in the direction of becoming a survivor by becoming actively involved in your own healing.
- We have talked a lot about what has happened to you, but not a lot about you. I want you to go over these pages and circle the drawings that best reflect who you are. You can circle as many as apply to you.

Following this activity place all pages in front of the parent. The parent is then asked to look at the pages, not what was circled, but what this activity "tells" the parent. The intervenor then supports the following:
- As I look at what you circled, I'm impressed by the fact that there are many parts that make you, who you are today.
- Following a trauma sometimes all you see, and all others see as they look at you and relate to you is "you the victim". The fact is, no matter how terrifying your experience was, it was only one part of your life, only part of your identity. There are many parts that make you "YOU".

Generally this activity solidifies the cognitive shift from victim to survivor and, at a sensory level, helps the parent experience a renewed sense of power and safety, two critical elements of healing. This is the same activity used with adolescents.

Session Four

Session four directs itself to creating a safe place. Survivor activities continue to help move the parent from a passive to active involvement in her own healing process. Sensory relief and empowerment activities build on the gains made in previous sessions.

The objectives of this session are:
- To continue to identify survivor patterns and initiate the Survivor Plan;
- To expand and strengthen the parent's ability to create an internal sense of safety.

Becoming a Survivor

The parent is asked to review the victim thinking checklist completed in the previous session to change and or add to victim thought patterns previously checked. The parent is also asked to complete another checklist, *Thoughts That Weigh Me Down*. This checklist is primarily designed to identify the possibility of suicidal responses that may have developed following the trauma. Thoughts such as "There is nothing else I can do." and "There's no point in trying anymore." can suggest a loss of hope and suicidal potential. If one has remained in the "victim state" for a prolonged period of time, powerlessness can turn to hopelessness and subsequent suicidal behavior. Although research on the correlation between PTSD and suicide is limited, practitioners must be careful to evaluate for possible suicidal thinking in those struggling to get past their victimization.

Following the identification of victim thinking, work begins on cognitively reframing victim thought patterns into survivor thought patterns using the *Survivor Thinking Checklist*. The *Survivor Checklist* reframes each victim thought pattern. This activity of reframing is very cognitive. Remember, however, that the parent has in previous sessions experienced what it means to be a survivor. This readies the parent to more easily make the necessary cognitive shifts in thinking. The parent is encouraged with the following reframing:

- This is an ongoing process. It doesn't happen immediately. (This segment is repeated. Repetition can be beneficial for victims to help overcome filtering or blocking of cognitive material.)
- The way we think does drive how we behave just as emotions, like fear, drive how we react. There is a time in life when we simply must commit ourselves to thinking differently about our situation, if we want that situation to change. This is one of those critical times.

- To change the way we think and ultimately act, we must consciously work at repeating these survivor thoughts to ourselves.
- This is important. We are not minimizing the pain of your experience. The memory of what happened will always be there. What we are doing is diminishing the hold that experience has on you. (Reframing) You have been wounded deeply. It will take time to heal. When you heal there will be a scar, in this case a memory, but the wound will no longer hurt at the level that it distracts, worries, or scares you. Your scar or memory will, in fact, in time remind you that you are a survivor, that there are other parts of your life now that hold your attention and are important.

Sensory Relief and Empowerment

In this activity a shift from the cognitive to the sensory is initiated. The parent is reminded of the relief she experienced in Session Two and then guided through the same activity as a starting point for additional sensory activities.

The following statements begin the activity:
- Becoming a survivor is partly a feeling experience. In other words thinking like a survivor is only part of reclaiming your life. You felt your trauma in your body - the pain, the hurt, the fear, the worry are triggered by sensory memories of that experience. Certain sounds, things you hear, smells and people you see can trigger those trauma memories and reactions.
- You need to know that you can relieve yourself or gain control of these reactions when they do appear. You remember in our Second Session we had you draw the funest, happiest, most pleasurable time you could recall. Remember what happened to the earlier physical reactions you were having from drawing about your experience? They weren't as bad, moved or were no longer present. What I want to do is teach you to "call up" that safe place; go to that safe place whenever you experience trauma reactions. The more you do this, the less powerful those trauma reactions will become. It's power will become your power.

Once the activity is completed the ability to "go to" this safe place is reinforced. An additional activity is then initiated. This time the parent is asked to pick one part of her trauma experience that she will think about and then describe. This will return some of the trauma feelings after which she is directed to return to her safe place. This reinforces the power the parent has to control some of the trauma reactions.

The degree of safety (relief) will vary. Cognitive reframing is important to normalize reactions of the parent. The parent is reminded that trauma is only one part of her life. She is told that at times getting to a safe place can actually trigger other trauma memories as a way of having another chance to now make sense of them.

These series of activities are important in preparation for dealing with the often intense reactions of anger, accountability and worry. They are designed to give the parent the empowerment needed to approach these difficult reactions as a survivor. The ability to make choices regarding anger and worry are critical to healing. Victims often are consumed by their worry and anger. To begin to find relief from and some control over these reactions, the parent must view herself as a survivor and not as a victim.

Session Five

This session identifies *Healing Benchmarks for Survivors* and addresses anger and revenge.

It's objectives are to:
- Identify ways the parent is doing better, and
- Identify, normalize and cognitively reframe issues of anger and revenge.

Healing Benchmarks

This activity allows the parent to again focus on the "survivor" inside. Eighteen different benchmarks are provided. The parent is told that any one item reflects a survivor response and with that response an internal healing is taking place. The parent is reminded that the wounds of the traumatic experience will always be remembered, but as a survivor the remembering, in time, will be manageable and, in fact, redefine life.

Anger - Revenge

SITCAP is not designed to treat rage. Rage is the result of multiple or long-term victimization during which one is left unprotected and/or the victimization gone unrecognized. Rage is rarely the result of a singular trauma. Rage manifests itself in behavior destructive to self and, at times, others. In less obvious behavior, rage shows itself in poor work history and poor relationships that are generally confrontive, filled with sudden burst of anger, often with no warning. It is dehumanizing and very threatening to its victims, emotionally and physically. Problems with authority, poor driving records, substance abuse, verbal abuse, threats to harm others, assaultive history, and fixation on revenge are potential indicators of rage. A quieter form of rage refers to the individual who appears depressed, victimized, blames others, cannot accept help. At times this quieter form can involve suicide - a form of aggression turned against oneself.

This is not an all inclusive definition of rage, but does alert the trauma intervenor to the importance of distinguishing between anger and rage. Anger is usually directed at a specific incident, where as rage has a long history. Rage dictates long-term treatment inclusive of psychotherapy, analysis, body work and in some cases medication.

This program focuses on anger resulting from traumatization. It is driven by a sense of powerlessness. Once empowered, trauma-driven anger diminishes. Should it be determined that the parent has "rage" problems, referral for long term psychotherapy is recommended.

In this activity the parent is asked to draw a picture of the person or thing that caused this trauma to happen. Specific trauma questions are asked to generate details, but also to identify the extent of the anger and whether the parent is able to control that anger. If the trauma was of a violent nature, it is not uncommon for victims to identify with their aggressor. This is one way to regain the very power that was taken from them. Questions related to their behavior when frustrated and upset can reveal the level of control or potential for self destructive, violent behavior.

Initial questions address the reaction not the outcome. Examples are: "Do you find yourself scared by how angry you get?" or, "Do you find yourself easily irritated?" and, "Do you find you can't allow yourself to think about how mad you are, for fear that you will lose control?" Should the answers to these types of questions be affirmative, further evaluation of potential violence is necessary. Criteria from the DSM-IV and other profiles are used to determine the need for more intense psychotherapy.

For the majority of trauma victims, trauma-driven anger is an attempt to re-experience power at a sensory level or to avoid the fear and terror associated with the vulnerability of feeling powerless over ones self and the immediate world outside the 'self.' The entire SITCAP intervention is a process of empowerment experienced first at a sensory level, then at a cognitive level. This then makes post-traumatic stress behavioral responses to frustration and anger a bit easier for the parent to engage.

The parent is directed in sensory activities as well as cognitive reframing. Suggestions are provided for dealing with frustration as well as managing stress levels. Anger is only introduced in the fifth session after the parent has had an opportunity to experience some level of relief from her fears as well as some renewed sense of power over those reactions triggered by the trauma. Not every victim will have major issues with anger and revenge. For some this may become a primary response. Additional treatment may be necessary, inclusive of medication to offset the chemical imbalances (depletion of catecholamines, serotonin and other neurotransmitters) that can cause mood swings, irritability and aggressive outbursts.

In the SITCAP model, work with subsequent sessions continues, even though additional work with anger is determined necessary. The remaining sessions are important to complete because they can help alleviate other anxieties and continue to strengthen the survivor response. This can, in fact, restore the energy needed to thereafter address the difficulties with anger or other problems.

Session Six

This session targets worry. Currently the relationship between worry and trauma is seldom addressed in the literature. References are made to worries following trauma, especially following catastrophic incidents such as hurricanes and floods. Worries often relate to the loss of shelter, food, clothing or in cases of violence that the same may happen again. What has not been closely examined has been the relationship between the overall reduction of worry and the comparable subsequent reduction of trauma severity levels.

The National Institute for Trauma and Loss in Children (TLC) has found in it's case studies that as the level of worry declines so too does the level of severity of reactions experienced. More formalized research is needed to account for variable influences, but patterns are sufficient enough to warrant focus on worry as part of trauma intervention.

Session Six has five activities: identifying existing worries, level of severity, likelihood of the worry happening, what can be done, and cognitive reframing.

The objectives of this session are:
- To identify major worries since the trauma;
- To determine factors of the worries that are realistically likely to occur;
- To problem solve identified worries;
- To cognitively reframe the parent's negative worries.

Identifying Worries

The reaction of worry is normalized for the parent. A worry checklist helps the parent identify ways in which worry occupies their energy and directs their behavior. Developing rituals, having to be near the phone, feeling that something else terrible is going to happen, worrying about not being able to stop the worry are some of the manifestations of worry the parent has the opportunity to identify.

Level or Severity and Likelihood Worry Will Happen

The parent is asked to identify her specific worries. A four level scale of severity is presented to the parent. Each of the worries are placed at the severity level determined by the parent. Another scale is used to rate the likelihood that a worry will become reality.

What Can Be Done

Once determined the severest worries are addressed first. The question, "What might be the hardest part for you should this worry become real?", is used to identify what "fuels" the worry. The entire process helps the parent externalize and concretize her worries. Now the parent can clearly see the elements of her worries and at a sensory level begin to feel more in control and less anxious about what, until now, has not been given a language.

The final step in this process is to help the parent role play what can be done to prepare for the reality that the worst may happen. This is an amazingly powerful activity because it gives the survivor choices, and with choices comes renewed power.

Cognitive Reframing

The final process for the intervenor is to cognitively reframe the way the parent responds to worry.

The work the parent has done up to this point has been designed to move her from victim to survivor. Her survivor perspective will help give her a different view of the future and her ability to deal with her biggest worries. As the intervenor you will still need to help shape how she does view herself in relationship to future trauma and her worries becoming a reality. The following are some cognitive reframing statements that can help.

- When someone is extremely worried about a present or potentially future situation, it is like tunnel vision. They anticipate, or are focused on, only one outcome and that outcome is given power by fear and or a sense of powerlessness. We know this is part of responding to life as a victim, not as a survivor.
- There is no way to predict whether our worries will ever become realities.
- Often our worries disappear because we and the conditions around us change.
- Worries are like storms. Storms never last. They come. They go. So too do worries. Some storms cause little damage; some cause great damage. That is

not something we can necessarily control. The only thing we can control is what we do after the storm leaves or the worry becomes a reality. Sometimes we can make repairs for ourselves; sometimes we need to call for the roofers, the plumbers, the electrician. Sometimes we can repair what happens to us alone, but sometimes we need to call for help. Just as we survive the storms, we can survive the worries.

- A crisis, just like worry, is a danger or an opportunity. If we do nothing, seek no help, it consumes us and takes control of our life. It can be an opportunity to learn what to do should similar incidents happen in the future. It's an opportunity to find inner strength that has never been tested. It's an opportunity to become stronger as a survivor and in time become less frightened of all the unfairness life can throw at us.
- We can't control a worry; we can only prepare for it and know that should our worry become a reality, we are ready to take whatever measures are needed to survive its challenges as well.
- As a survivor, you will know there is more to life than worry; there are challenges and rewards for accepting those challenges. There is fear, but there is also the other side of fear - freedom: freedom to be you, freedom to always have the final choice of what you are going to do for yourself, each and everyday of your life, despite the challenges of that day. Since the worry is not likely to go away soon, and since you can't control it, only prepare for it if it does happen. You can let it be while you get on with other things in your life.

Should this entire focus on worry be experienced as all too overwhelming or simply not helpful, it may be an indication that:
- Chemical imbalances caused by the trauma are blocking or preventing a reduction of the arousal response;
- The trauma experience was preceded by previous disorders and or triggered additional disorders such as depression. In either case further evaluation for medication and/or existing disorders would be recommended.

The reality is that diagnostic tools can identify the presence of PTSD and indicate a level of severity. What assessment tools cannot do is determine the response to intervention. SITCAP is structured to be experienced as a safe process, as one that can help bring a sense of relief, a renewed sense of control, understanding and a reordering of the experience in a way that is manageable. The fact is not every trauma victim will necessarily feel safe enough to engage in these activities. It is important to communicate support and, that any time, the parent can always return to address her trauma.

Session Seven

Session Seven provides the opportunity to evaluate the reduction of trauma reactions and or the absence of change or increase in levels of severity. It provides the parent with an opportunity to revisit the experience in order to complete the story and identify areas that need additional clarification or attending. The focus on being a survivor continues, and the parent revisits *Healing Benchmarks* to expand the areas and ways they are healing. The parent also is asked to identify the change experienced between the first session and this session.

The objectives of this session are:
- To evaluate current gains and changes since the initial session;
- To review the major focal points of each session in order to discover forgotten parts, spend time on facts needing additional attention;
- To reorder the experience so that it is now manageable;
- To find meaning or purpose from the experience;
- To end the story and move from being a victim to being a survivor.

Evaluation

The parent is asked to complete the *Parent PTSD Questionnaire*. This is the same tool used at the initial session. The parent is told that some of her reactions are likely to be less severe, some significantly less severe. The parent is also told that some reactions may have stayed the same and this is normal as some changes may take more time. Knowing which reactions have stayed the same, however, can help to determine what else may be needed to help. The results will be reviewed in the final session.

Reviewing the Story

At this point in the intervention process, the parent has likely found some relief and experienced a renewed sense of power and a different understanding of her reactions to her traumatic experience. It is likely that her arousal state has decreased and she is feeling a bit safer with her emotions and the trauma reactions that were endured by her experience.

It is very beneficial to take the parent through the major themes and focal points of each session at this time. It allows her to now see her entire experience, all its parts as a whole rather than fragmented memories and thoughts. It provides an opportunity to still discover forgotten parts, return to parts that need additional attention, and most importantly, to now reframe her experience in a way that is manageable. It is important to have an ending to the trauma experience, an end to the story; so a new beginning as a survivor can begin. This review will likely take the entire session. If more time is needed it can be concluded in the next session. This is a very critical session; as much time as needed is to be taken.

All drawings and activity worksheets are placed on a table for the parent to view. Trauma-specific questions are asked to narrow the focus.

Examples of these questions include the following:
- As you look at your drawings/activity worksheets and all the different parts of your story, what stands out the most?
- Are there any parts of the experience, any details not in your drawings/worksheets, that need to be added? If so, go ahead and draw them. (If parts are added be sure to get the details, the "story" for each part and how it is significant).
- As you look at all of your drawings/worksheets what surprises you the most?
- Which drawing/worksheet now means the most to you or is the most important? What makes it important?

- As you think about it now, how has the experience changed your view of your life?
- Finally, as you think about it now, what positive has come out of this traumatic experience?

This process helps to solidify what the parent has learned at a sensory level as well as cognitive level. Because it is their story what has been learned is empowering and supports the survivor attitude even when the parent is in need of additional intervention. The healing experience is continued by moving into a review of *Survivor Thinking and Healing Benchmarks*.

Survivor Focus - Healing Benchmarks

The parent is directed to review these checklists and to double check those items that reflect their survivor view and the healing that has taken place. Often new thought patterns and healing benchmarks are also identified. Having the parent actively make the effort to review and check each item keeps her actively involved in her own healing and more open to her accepting any new cognitive understanding of her experience. The session ends with the following reframing:

- You certainly have worked hard. Where you were when we began is not where you are now. You have changed. You have changed the way you think, the way you feel. You have moved from feeling powerless and overwhelmed to feeling a renewed sense of power and control and some relief. I only showed you the way. You did the work. You really are a survivor.
- Things will never be the same, but change sometimes takes us places we never dreamed were possible. Life will always have challenges. Hopefully, future ones will not be as difficult and as frightening as this past one. I know life can be unfair, but I really believe now that the survivor in you will survive what life sends you. You really do deserve to be applauded for how hard you have fought for yourself.

Session Eight

This session helps the parent complete their *Survivor Plan*, allows for a final review and the parents decision to continue with additional intervention if needed. And, being the last session, how one says good bye is important.

The objectives of this session are:
- To review the Parent's PTSD Questionnaire score.
- To prepare the parent for the possibility of needing help in the future.
- To complete and present the parent with the Survivor Plan.

Reviewing the Process

Scoring of the *Parents PTSD Questionnaire* completed in Session Seven is reviewed at the beginning of the session. Support is given for the parent's effort throughout the process. Support is given for the reduction of reactions. It is important to tell the parent that change will continue beyond intervention and that surviving is a life long activity simply because life has its good moments and not so good moments.

Some reactions may take longer to diminish. If any reaction is interfering with everyday functions such as work performance, family relationships or sleep, additional evaluation and or intervention should be recommended as medication and/or additional intervention may be needed.

Survivor Plan

With the help of completed activity worksheets the majority of this session is spent on completing the *Survivor Plan*. Examples of the area covered by the *Survivor Plan* are listed on the following page:

- I know I am healing and will continue to heal because: (using the *Healing Benchmarks for Survivors* write down the double checked items.)
- The most effective way for me to manage my anger is... (use suggestions identified in Session Five.)

- As a survivor I will remind myself of the following: (using the *Survivor Thinking Checklist* completed in Session Seven, write down the double checked statements).
- Worry follows trauma, but as a survivor I will continue to work on the three ways I'm going to prepare should my biggest worry become a reality. (Write these down.)
- As a survivor I remember that trauma is only one part of my life. I have many different parts and know I will develop even newer parts because I am a survivor. The best thing I like about me now is...
- As a surviving parent, I also realize there are likely to be future difficulties I may not be certain how to best handle. As a survivor I do know that my greatest asset is having the courage and the choice to call for help.

Saying Good Bye

When saying goodbye, it is important to prepare the parent for the future. Cognitive reframing is part of the process. SITCAP scripts reframing to ensure the critical components of recovery are addressed. Examples include:
- You have done a lot of hard work, are feeling more in control, and have power over your trauma. You have a *Survivor Plan* and will continue to grow stronger as a survivor.
- Life is life and there could be additional crisis in your life. I think you will survive those too, but that doesn't mean you might not need some help with them as well. Everyone needs help at times. A survivor knows it is not only okay, but smart to ask for help when attempts to solve the problem are not working. I just want to be sure you hear this loud and clear.
- There is sometimes a tendency to think that you have failed when faced with additional trauma. Just remember this is the victim talking. The survivor knows there will always be times when help is needed simply because different situations present new or complicated issues never experienced. This is life.
- I want to again thank you for all of your hard work, for what you shared with me and for your determination to heal yourself.

Referral/Continuation

The need for referral or continuation of additional intervention if necessary will be easily recognized by the parent. The parent has choices. The one choice is to continue intervention. It is important to provide a time frame for that intervention of 4-8 weeks followed by a reevaluation. The parent also has the option to take a break - get some distance. The parent can work on their *Survivor Plan* and see if reactions become less intense. Again, provide a 4-8 week time period. Time does heal and many parents do well when on their own. The parent understands that if reactions do not lessen in frequency or if additional traumas occur, intervention can again be initiated. The most important factor is experiencing this process as a positive one that has helped them find some relief, renewed empowerment and a different understanding of what happened to them. These are the factors that encourage the parent, as a survivor, to call for help in the future.

Adult Case Example

This example focuses on the importance of drawing and the telling of the story. It illustrates the value of providing victims the opportunity to make us a witness to their experiences - to see it and sense it as they did in the past and now in the present. It also illustrates that once actually involved, victims can continue their own healing process. Finally, this case illustrates that not all traumatization needs extensive, long term intervention.

The Persian Gulf War left many families traumatized. This example dramatically illustrates the strength of the healing process when the victim is provided an opportunity to safely tell her story in a way that words often cannot describe. It is an example of how, once actively involved in this process, the victim (survivor) can continue the healing process on her own and how relief can be realized in a short period.

While the family was at home, Iraqi soldiers invaded the home and beat the husband and teenage son in front of the rest of the family. After the beating they dragged the father and son off as prisoners, the majority of whom were then butchered and killed. The atrocities of this war were extreme. The son later escaped. The father's body was discovered and identified almost one year later.

The mother was relieved that her son escaped, the wife was devastated. Her husband had been missing for one year, then to receive the call that his body may have been discovered left her in great pain. His tortured state induced intense reactions. This intervention was provided approximately five months after the body was identified. There was certainly a heroic part within this woman. She had volunteered to be a part of a new program initiated by Kuwait's Social Development Office to bring mental health assistance to its victimized families. She volunteered to participate in an abbreviated demonstration of the SITCAP model in which she was asked to draw and tell her story.

This intervention began at an evening session. When asked to draw a picture that she could tell a story about she drew her husbands face (Plate 15). What was unusual about this experience was that this was part of a training we were conducting over several weeks, meeting day and evening. Each day she carried with her what we came to know as *The Book of Martyrs*. Every page of this 200 page book had photographs of the war's tortured victims of all ages inclusive of young children. She had the book with her at all times. She was literally carrying the trauma memories of her husband's torture with her everyday. This became very significant.

Plate 15

After drawing her husband's face, we asked for trauma-specific details of the incident as well as the picture. Skin had been torn away, teeth were missing. It was as if his face was frozen in unbearable pain. During this process most who were observing assumed his eyes were closed. However, no assumptions are made in this process. All details of the drawing are questioned. "What is this line? Tell me about his mouth." When she was asked about his eyes she replied, "They were gone." His eyes had been gouged out.

This one response is a good example of the importance of detail and how it can "make sense" of the victim's responses.

As the narrative continued she was asked to draw a picture of her brother, who was most helpful to her at the time she had to identify her husband's body. (Plate 15.1) is a picture of her brother. She was again asked specific questions related to where in her body she experienced the hurt the most, as well as questions about the drawing. Highlighted are her brother's eyes. She was asked about his eyes. He was wearing sun glasses in this drawing. Emerging was a theme focused on the eyes. That theme is revealed as the story (narrative) is told. It is not important to ask "why" in attempts to understand. The understanding, the meaning will be revealed as the story is told. Because she had not drawn her husband's entire body, she was asked to do so (Plate 15.2). This represents a pivotal point in the intervention and also illustrates that when we let the story be told, we learn.

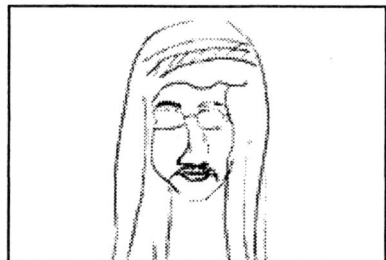

Plate 15.1

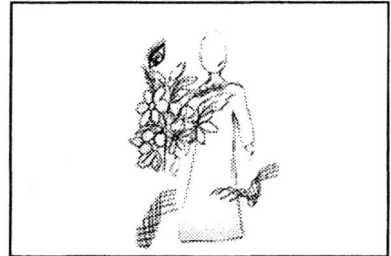

Plate 15.2

She did not draw his face. When asked, "I notice there is no face. Can you draw in his face?" her response was that she did not want to. We don't attempt to explore why, but accept that what is provided is what can be provided. By accepting her not wanting to draw this detail, we support the effort to keep her at wherever her "safe place" is at the time. She went on to describe details of his tortured body. The flowers were drawn as she talked. For some, the repetition of drawing creates a sensation of safety and comfort. The flowers represented the flower of hope in Kuwait. The other lines were just "doodles".

What is prominent in this drawing is the eye in the upper left side. When asked about the eye, she replied, "It's really strange. Ever since this all happened, whenever I scribble I find myself drawing eyes." In trauma work of this type metaphors emerge, themes in the drawings themselves emerge. Her husband's eyes were shut and missing. Her brother's eyes were covered with sun glasses. Her husband's full body drawing had no eyes, yet in the same drawing there was a wide open eye.

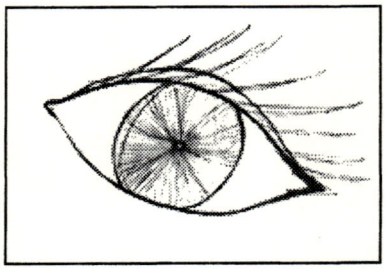

Plate 15.3

At this point she was asked to use a full sheet of paper to draw an eye. She was then instructed to sit quietly for two minutes but during that time to trace the eye continuously (Plate 15.3) letting her mind go wherever it desired.

This continual psychomotor activity will sometimes trigger additional memories. It can intensify sensations as well as bring release and comfort. She was told that whatever memories she might have would be hers to keep unless she wished to share any afterwards. Physically her face appeared to reveal a remembering of additional details. When asked if there was anything she would like to share she said no, while at the same time wiping a tear from her eye.

Plate 15.4

At this point she was asked if she could draw a picture of her husband with his eyes open, as he was before his death. Her immediate response was, "no". She indicated that she could draw other faces, but not her husband. She was then asked to draw someone else's face (Plate 15.4). The reason for this was the fact that this was where she brought us in her story. When asked if she could tell us about the person she just drew, she said that she couldn't because it wasn't anyone she knew, just a face. She was asked if she could then draw a picture of her husband with his eyes open and quietly say all the things she wished she could have said before he was tortured and dragged away. She could not. In grief work the effort is to reestablish a living memory that is a positive. Her living memory was of her tortured husband's body, his pain and her terror.

The evening was going to be ending shortly, so she was taken to pleasant memories; a safe place, before ending. She was told that we would finish the next morning and that if she needed to talk at anytime through the night because of memories or sensations this experience triggered, she could call without hesitation. She did not call.

The next morning when she came in, she put the *Book of Martyrs* she had carried with her for weeks on our table and took her seat. There was no idea as to what this meant. When we began she indicated that throughout the evening she had numerous memories but was not sure if some were false memories, "her imagination." She then indicated that she called a number of friends and family members to validate her memories. In other words, she remained actively involved in her own healing process. She shared the new information with us, which helped to fill in the missing parts of her story. It was all making sense for her and for us. There was an obvious change in the way she was presenting. The tension had left. There was a relief. That relief in all probability related to a number of factors; being able to fill in the gaps, making sense of some of her reactions, having a new understanding of trauma, obtaining new information and validating the information.

Plate 15.5

At this time, she was then asked if she could draw a picture of her husband with his eyes open and then quietly, to herself, say all the things she would have liked to have said if she had the chance before he was dragged away from her forever. There was no hesitation. Plate 15.5 is the living memory of her husband that overnight had now become her focus. She asked if she might tell us aloud the things she would have said. It was a very tender, loving reuniting with her husband, not as a victim, but as a living memory of the love they had shared.

In a short period of time this woman went from being "stuck" in her trauma and literally carrying with her the horrible trauma she endured by the tortured state of her husband; to now letting go, giving us the trauma (the book) and replacing it with all that was good about her husband and their relationship.

Certainly, not all interventions see this kind of outcome over a short period. It does demonstrate that without this kind of structured, trauma focused intervention that provided her an opportunity to make us a witness to her trauma in ways that words cannot do, she would have continued in her trauma state, controlled by the memories of her tortured husband; the visual memories as documented in *The Book of Martyrs*.

CHAPTER NINE
Debriefing
Trauma-specific Intervention for Schools and Agencies

These trauma debriefing interventions are part of the SITCAP model. They address the unique intervention needs of schools, students, staff. They have been specifically designed to meet the very unique administrative needs, management, and diverse populations of the school environment. The first two days following a critical incident are the most chaotic. Shock, denial and sensory implosion leave survivors in a state of crisis. Crisis intervention is appropriate these first two days. Also appropriate and needed in those first two days is an organized response which involves classroom presentations. By the third and fourth days initial reactions begin to change. Debriefing for the most exposed is needed at that time. In six to eight weeks following the crisis additional interventions will be needed for some. Delayed reactions can lead to the need for intervention months later.

The Debriefing Model discussed in this chapter is a variation of the Critical Incident Stress Debriefing (CISD) model developed by Jeffrey Mitchell (1991) for use following disasters to assist rescue workers, medical and law enforcement personnel involved with remaining survivors or victims.

The Debriefing Models to be discussed are the result of field testing, discussions and consultations conducted by The National Institute for Trauma and Loss in Children (1998) with over 1,500 professionals in school and agency settings. The models address the unique needs of schools and agencies. Trauma Debriefing, Classroom Defusing, Classroom Presentations, Operational Debriefing and

Debriefing for Team Members address the different needs of the students/clients of various ages, the distinct needs of the most exposed and least exposed staff, and the distinct needs of the crisis team members. Likewise, they address the needs of all staff in relationship to the system in which they must perform during the crisis. Finally, they address the informational and educational needs of students and clients which are outside the realm of debriefing and defusing.

This chapter cannot detail the actual stages of the five models to be reviewed but will answer the many questions professionals in schools and agencies have about the process, its initiation and application. This information is difficult to find in publication at this time. The Institute's *Trauma Debriefing for Schools and Agencies Handbook* does provide detailed descriptions of each model and the associated stages. Before reviewing the models, whom they are for, when they are initiated, how they are conducted, participant issues, duration, purposes and format, it is important to answer several questions about debriefing.

About Debriefing

What is debriefing?

Petersen and Straub (1994) define debriefing as "the process of putting the incident (trauma) and the individual's reactions in perspective." Johnson (1993) specifically describes debriefing as "a form of crisis intervention...Individuals can air their perceptions of the event, their reactions to it, and their concerns for the future in a structured, supportive context." Mitchell (1991 CISD Video) defines debriefing as "a group process designed to mitigate the impact of the event and to accelerate normal recovery." Meichenbaum (1994) describes debriefing as "a group method that helps the workers to process and defuse their emotional reactions by means of educational, preventative, and supportive process. It is designed to prevent unnecessary complications that follow from exposure to disasters." Steele (1999) details specific debriefing strategies unique to schools and agencies, their limitation, special needs and diverse population.

Debriefing dates back to the early 1900's when used in the military. Mitchell is credited with adapting military protocol to fit the needs of emergency health care workers and rescue personnel. In the 1970's he titled his model Critical Incident Stress Debriefing (CISD).

Other models have been developed since the CISD model. Armstrong (1991), Griffin (1987), Raphael (1986), and Wagner (1979) have all developed models, but Mitchell's model receives the most attention.

The Mitchell CISD process has been altered by others for adaptation in school settings as well. Petersen and Straub (1994) for example, recommend that no more than fifteen - twenty people be debriefed at one time. They identify five phases of the process. Johnson (1993) suggests that up to 40 students can be debriefed at one time with the basic rule of "take as long as it takes" to complete. He identifies five stages to the process as well, which were adapted from Mitchell's seven stage model.

What are It's Objectives?

Debriefing is a group intervention process whose objectives are: to provide participants the opportunity to share information related to the details of the incident; to identify the cognitive, behavioral, emotional, and physical reactions to it; to alter, as needed, perceptions and understanding of the incident and reactions to it; to find some relief from the experience via participant support, normalization of reactions and corrections of misperceptions; to prepare participants for reactions they might experience in the future; and to suggest ways they can cope with current and possible future reactions.

What is It's Overall Purpose?

The purpose of TLC's debriefing models is to accelerate healing from the terror induced by traumatic incidents, to prevent the formation of posttraumatic stress disorder (PTSD), and to be used as a learning tool to better prepare victims, survivors, schools and agencies for future critical incidents.

What Type of Incident Requires Debriefing?

Debriefing is generally applied to those situations which induce acute stress. By definition this would be sudden, unexpected, unusual human experience. The incident would have posed a serious threat to one's life or physical integrity, or to the life of a family member or close friend or to one's surrounding environment (home, school, workplace). This would also include those individuals who were witnesses to such an incident.

TLC's research (Raider, Steele and Santiago, 1999) found high levels of trauma severity in children exposed to murder, suicide, domestic violence, physical/sexual abuse, car fatalities, house fires, drowning, critical injuries due to environmental tragedies or accidents, terminal illness, separation from a parent, divorce, living with substance abusing parents, etc.

The research also found high levels of trauma following life threatening incidents such as floods, hurricanes, workplace violence, community violence, explosions, fires, overturned school buses, hostage situations, kidnappings, suicides, and other sudden deaths. All of these incidents could require debriefing.

Hobfoll (1994) has designed a model in which he identifies four sources of stress arising from a disaster: a) objects, b) conditions, c) personal characteristics, d) energies.

<u>Objects</u> involve the loss of our personal possessions. At a personal level, this could include the loss of our car, home, etc.; and, at a community level, less access to roads, shelters, emergency equipment, etc.

<u>Conditions</u> which can be lost at a personal level could include our social ties and roles (employment, parenthood, marriage) and, at the community level, the loss of the opportunity to work, to secure emergency services, etc.

<u>Personal characteristics</u> which can be lost include the inner strengths of the individual, e.g. self-esteem, self-efficacy; and those "outer" attributes which reflect inner strengths e.g. social skills, specialized work skills, etc. At a community level such characteristics could include community pride and competence.

<u>Energies</u> at a personal level refer to resources such as money, food, knowledge, etc. At a community level these refer to community resources such as money, transportation, safety, how the community (at a government level) responds to a crisis.

This model reminds us that a trauma can be created not only from involvement with the specific incident itself but also through the additional losses it can create at a community level. It is important to keep in mind that it is not the incident itself which induces acute stress, but the level of vulnerability and powerlessness of the child or adult at the time of the incident, which can leave him exposed to post-traumatic stress.

What are the differences between grief and trauma, acute stress, posttraumatic stress?

There are significant differences between grief and trauma, acute stress and posttraumatic stress disorder.

Debriefing generally is reserved for trauma victims who are experiencing acute stress. To appreciate the debriefing process it is important to understand the differences between grief and trauma and then the differences between acute stress and posttraumatic stress disorder (PTSD).

GRIEF	**TRAUMA**
Generalized reaction is SADNESS	Generalized reaction is TERROR
Grief reactions stand alone	Trauma reactions generally include grief reactions
Grief reactions are generally known to the public and the professional	Trauma reactions especially in children are largely unknown to the public and often professionals
In grief, most can generally talk about what happened	In trauma, most do not want to talk about what happened
In grief, pain is the acknowledgement of the loss	In trauma, pain triggers tremendous terror and an overwhelming sense of powerlessness and loss of safety
In grief, anger is generally non-destructive and non-assaultive	In trauma, anger often becomes assaultive even after non-violent trauma
In grief, guilt says "I wish I would/would not have..."	Trauma guilt says, "It was my fault. I could have prevented it" and "It should have been me instead."
Grief generally does not attack nor "disfigure" our self image	Trauma generally attacks, distorts and "disfigures" our self image
In grief, dreams tend to be of the deceased	In trauma, dreams are about self as potential victim
Grief generally does not involve trauma reactions	Trauma involves grief reactions in addition to trauma-specific reactions

The chart on the previous page compares grief and trauma differences. It is easy to see that at the core of trauma is terror. When we are in terror, everything feels chaotic and out of control. A structured debriefing process is designed to minimize the chaos and help participants regain a sense of control over the chaos and terror.

Acute stress refers to the first four weeks following the initiation of the trauma inducing incident. The reactions of acute stress are similar to posttraumatic stress (PTSD). The reactions in these first four weeks often further intensify the victim's level of anxiety because the victim is unfamiliar with these reactions. They are frequently experienced as unusual and abnormal.

The major difference between acute stress and PTSD is a period of four weeks. When acute stress reactions continue beyond the initial four week period, PTSD becomes the diagnosis.

It is argued by some that this four week criteria is not necessarily a valid time frame when the critical incident is followed by additional situations which prevent the return of previous support systems. Following a hurricane or severe flooding communities can be left without water, food, shelter, electricity or access in and out of the community because of damaged or impassable roads. The absence of these otherwise normal resources and infrastructures can delay healing and perhaps prolong the acute stress period.

In school environments the trauma impact of suicide and other incidents can be prolonged by additional suicides or subsequent incidents. The death of a student in a fatal car crash just days before prom night, for example, can trigger a variety of complex and conflictual issues that can delay or prolong reactions. Media attention often intensifies reactions and triggers additional reactions because of the reporting of inaccurate information and the intrusiveness of reporters. Factors that develop after the initial incident, therefore, should be taken into consideration when thinking of the duration of the acute stress period.

Does debriefing work?

Clinical experience has shown that debriefing accelerates healing and lessens the severity of symptoms. In general, participants are immensely grateful for the opportunity to share the details of their ordeal, to listen to the experience of others, to discover they are not alone in their reactions, and to learn that what they are experiencing is normal. In the author's experience, there is no doubt that debriefing helps accelerate healing, restores inner control and order, and provides relief from stress.

Actual research always lags behind clinical experiences. This certainly does not invalidate the process. There have been very few studies to document the impact of debriefing on trauma victims. Definitive conclusions are not possible due to sample size and the variety of debriefing processes. Despite these limitations, findings do suggest that debriefing can reduce trauma reactions.

Yule (1992) studied the impact of debriefing on survivors of the Jupiter cruise ship sinking in 1988. Two seamen, one teacher and one pupil were killed when the Jupiter was sunk by a tanker. There were 400 children and 90 teachers aboard. Many had to jump into the sea. Nearly half of the surviving children experienced PTSD. They ranged in age from 11-18 years old with most being between 14-15 years old. Debriefing was held ten days after the incident, and thereafter two small groups were run. Problem-solving strategies were added to the debriefing model. The children involved in the early intervention showed a reduction in symptoms nine months later. However, the problem with this study was that debriefing was not the only intervention provided.

Shalev (1994), Raphel et al. (1994), suggest that there is little systematic evidence such as controlled studies or long term follow up, to support the benefits of debriefing. In fact, McFarlane (1994) notes that "The few outcome studies of debriefing which have comparison groups suggest that these interventions may worsen the outcome of some of those participating rather than having the desired effect of lessening the distress of those involved."

McFarlane does go on to say that this concern must be placed alongside the strong perceptions that debriefing is helpful. Understanding that simple exposure to hearing of the details (Saigh, 1991) can induce trauma, one might expect an increase at least temporarily in stress levels and symptomatology. It is also important to understand that delayed reactions may account for this "worsening", not the debriefing itself. There is no way to predict who will or will not benefit from debriefing.

Pynoos (1994) reported the reduction of severe reactions in two classes of Armenian students involved in an earthquake. In addition to debriefing, students received 3-4 individual and group sessions over the next year and a half after the earthquake. Almost 92% of the children experienced a significant reduction in their trauma symptoms, which was said to be remarkable because of the "unremitting severity" of the disaster. However, because debriefing was not the only intervention used, it is impossible to draw conclusions about the effectiveness of debriefing by itself.

Does debriefing therefore work? Clinical experiences says "yes"; research is inconclusive. Meichenbaum (1994) reports "CISD may provide some immediate opportunities for victims to talk with one another, but it is unlikely to provide effective treatment for complex, ongoing or persistent problems that are a result of the disaster itself, pre-disaster vulnerabilities, or the variety of social conditions that survive it." Many participants of debriefing have supported its value to them. Perhaps its importance is the attention, education, and support it immediately provides victims and the opportunity to provide participants additional intervention as needed. Experience tells us that participants are far more likely to accept intervention brought to them than to actually pursue intervention on their own.

The TLC Institute has found it's debriefing strategies extremely beneficial for school staff, crisis teams and administrators. Its models help to identify ways administration can support its staff during the days following a critical incident as well as benefit crisis team members with both their personal reactions as well as their professional responses and issues arising from the systems responses.

What is the difference between debriefing and trauma intervention?

Debriefing does not utilize trauma-specific intervention processes like guided imagery, drawing, art activities, hypnosis, use of metaphors, etc. Debriefing's purpose is to acknowledge, share, empathize, reassure, and support. The purpose of trauma intervention is to explore, search for personal insight and meaning, focus on past trauma inducing memories triggered by the most recent event, and take the time needed to work through the most troubling issues triggered by the trauma experience. Debriefers act as a referral source for those needing intervention beyond the initial debriefing period. They are not necessarily clinically trained in psychology, social work or other graduate level clinical areas.

Who gets debriefed?

To understand who may need debriefing, it is critical to understand how we can become exposed to acute stress - PTSD reactions.

Exposure: There are four possible avenues of exposure, 1) as surviving victim - victims of physical/sexual abuse, other assaults, community violence, critical injuries, catastrophic situations, etc., 2) as witness to any potential trauma-inducing incident, violent or non-violent - murder, suicide, assault, car fatality, bus tragedy, house fire, drowning, etc., 3) being related to the victim - as a family member, friend, or peer. "Relationship" may also include one's personal identification with victims. Schwarz and Kowalski's (1991) study of 64 children following a school shooting showed that, irrespective of physical nearness to the event, emotional stress resulting from personal identification also led to PTSD); 4) verbal exposure - Saigh (1991) found that by listening to the details of traumatic experiences, traumatic stress reactions can be induced. This is especially true for professionals responsible for intervention with traumatized children. Vicarious traumatization is always a potential development. Children who are exposed to repeated media coverage of details and survivors understandably still may be exposed to prolonged and/or more intense trauma reactions.

Being "related to" and a "witness to" is far more frequent in today's technological society. Approximately six months after the Oklahoma bombing this author was speaking to a group of Head Start teachers. During the presentation, one of the teachers told the story of how her children spontaneously devised a game where one half of them took all their sleeping (floor) mats and covered themselves. The other half in pairs of two, one at a time would go over to the other children, lift up the mat, pick up the child under the mat and then escort that child over to the other side of the room by their indoor soccer nets. They did this until all the children under the mats were rescued and taken to the "safety nets". Afterward, they switched sides. Rescuers became victims trapped under the mats; victims were now rescuers.

By being witnesses to the tragedies of the bombing and seeing rescue workers carry out children their own ages from the rubble of the day care center, these preschool children identified with the victims and consequently needed to find a way at a sensory level to gain power over their fear.

Given the understanding of exposure, we could say, for example, that an entire school could need debriefing following a school bus accident or a suicide or some other critical incident. There is no argument following a critical incident that all children will need attention, information, education and an opportunity to ask questions and talk about what happened. However, not everyone will need to participate in the full debriefing process.

A distinction needs to be made between "classroom presentation" and debriefing. Classroom presentations when conducted appropriately, provide the majority of students the information and opportunities they need to cope successfully with the school's experience. Classroom presentations could be conducted for the entire student body in their classes immediately following the incident and then again to provide educational information related to the factors of the incident, ways to cope, etc. Following a classroom presentation, those children who have been identified by their behavior as needing additional help would be seen individually. They could then be evaluated for level of risk, need for debriefing and need of further services.

Debriefing is reserved for the most exposed. Initially, it includes those who witnessed the trauma or were surviving victims of the incident, were a family member or close friend of the victim or have a "perceived identity" with the victim. Others may be identified as needing debriefing but will initially need to be evaluated to determine what actually might be best for them. Keep in mind that debriefing is generally best initiated about 3 to 7 days following the incident, where as classroom work can be done immediately.

How long after an incident can debriefing be initiated? When is the best time to debrief?

Debriefing can be initiated between 24 to 72 hours. This is not always possible given the environmental and organizational issues at hand. In disaster situations it may be up to five days before debriefing groups are held simply because environmental issues, rescue efforts, finding shelter, etc. remain the priority.

Yule (1992) suggests that debriefing with children and adolescents is best done between 7-14 days following an incident. These authors would concur that this is the best time. The immediate needs are to obtain factual information, to restore some sense of order and safety, and to attempt to meet the first level responses of all involved.

Debriefing, however, if deemed critical, can be done a few hours after the incident (Pynoos and Eth, 1986). However, be prepared for the need to return in several days as the initial shock and denial may prohibit cognitive processing.

There is no data available supporting the optimal time to initiate the debriefing process. There are benefits to immediate as well as delayed debriefing. In fact, in this author's experience, debriefings can actually be conducted months, even years following critical incidents It is quite common that years later people will immediately return emotionally even physically to their experience as if it happened only a day earlier. This is also seen in professionals who were not debriefed after their involvement in responding to critical incidents as well as surviving victims left unattended.

There are several advantages to waiting a few days before initiating debriefing. First, it is easier to evaluate the overall reaction and stability of all involved. Second, it is easier to gather factual information. Third, it allows individuals the opportunity to rely on their own coping skills to better determine for themselves the need to be involved in debriefing. The same could be said for a school setting where hysterical contagion can make it difficult to determine who needs what services in the first few days.

The most critical component is follow-up. The reactions of acute stress are the same reactions of PTSD. The only difference is that the acute stress period is four weeks. If reactions continue beyond four weeks, the diagnosis is PTSD. Therefore, it is critical to return 6 - 10 weeks after the initial debriefing to identify those who have moved into PTSD.

How long does a debriefing session take?

Using the Mitchell model, debriefing can take as long as three hours. This time frame may prove difficult for school and at agency settings. Johnson (1993) suggests different durations for different developmental levels - preschool-K at 15-

30 minutes; lower elementary at 30 minutes - 1 hour; upper elementary at 30 minutes - 1 hour; junior high at 45 minutes - 1 1/2 hours; and high school at 1 - 2 hours.

However, it is important to note that the formal debriefing process is far too cognitive and structured for the preschool and lower elementary levels. This age level will respond more favorably to defusing activities along with some cognitive processing which makes for a longer session and possibly calls for two sessions. *Helping Children Feel Safe* is the TLC debriefing program for younger children.

It may be difficult to retain high school students as well as staff beyond two hours for debriefing. One wonders how much more can be processed and accomplished after two hours of intense sharing. Clinical experience tells us that after two hours of intense focus the mind and body begins to wander and seek distance from such intensity. The flooding of overwhelming reactions induces the risk of actually exacerbating the trauma condition.

If a debriefing session lasts beyond two hours it may be a signal that 1) there were too many people in the group; 2) a dominant participant was not managed appropriately; 3) the structure of the process was not properly followed. The caution about debriefing going beyond two hours is that it leaves too much room for emotions to become unraveled, for individuals to reveal far more than they intended, for debriefers to fall into the role of therapist rather than facilitator and educator.

The recommendation is that it is always better to return for a second session than to prolong the initial session. Remember part of the message debriefers want to convey to participants is that, as difficult as this has been, they are still capable of coping even when there may be additional issues that need to be taken up at an additional session.

How many people can be debriefed at one time?

There is disagreement in this area. Johnson (1993) suggests that entire classrooms can be debriefed. Petersen and Straub (1992) recommend a limit of 15-20 participants. Meichenbaum (1994), in his review of debriefing history and models suggest that 6-15 is the maximum.

The basic premise of debriefing is that each participant should have the opportunity to share the details of his experience -- what he saw and heard; his first thoughts; what surprised him about his reactions; all the physical and emotional reactions. This is done in stages with each person. For each of the 8-10 participants to answer all the questions will take approximately two hours. It is virtually impossible to debrief a group of 10 or more people and give each of them adequate time to share the details of his experience. Debriefing is not designed for larger groups. Working with larger groups demands different approaches such as the classroom presentations, operational debriefing and defusing models such as TLC's.

Debriefing is reserved for the most exposed. If there are more than 8-10 most exposed victims then initiate additional debriefing groups.

Should administrators or other officials be included with line staff?

No. It is best to debrief administrators and other officials separately. The issues are different. The relationships between line staff and administrators can be complex. All of this may inhibit self-disclosure by the staff.

In school settings it is not unusual to find administrators and line staff very supportive of one another. This is understandable since they have the welfare of the children as a focal point. They need to know that each participant will be treated equally and that the debriefing process is not about blame or responsibility. If the debriefers believe that the differences in position will not be a barrier to the process, then proceed. With these things in mind, successful debriefing can be accomplished with a mix of administrators and staff.

School environments are different than agency, organization and community environments. In agency and other settings it is advisable to group people by their position and/or role in the experience, for example witnesses, rescuers, administrators/supervisors, line staff, etc.

Can you have more than one session with the same people in one day?

Yes. As stated earlier, it is our belief that two hours is the optimal range of effectiveness to meet. At the same time, participants may need additional time. A morning meeting followed by an evening meeting would be appropriate. A one to two hour break may be sufficient when two hours simply is not enough time to complete the process.

The goal is to stabilize individuals as quickly as possible. Individuals are seen as often as necessary in the first several days.

Can the same people be debriefed over an extended period of time?

Yes. Pynoos and others have returned to the setting one year later to conduct debriefings. Community disasters, for example, deal with numerous external factors that can prolong recovery. Frequently there are ongoing reminders of the trauma. The type of disaster, extent of injuries, deaths, and the potential for reoccurrence can all have prolonged impact on survivors which necessitate further debriefing.

In school systems that have been exposed to multiple deaths over a period of months, one would anticipate the need to return for debriefing after each incident and again a month or two following the last incident. Pennebaker and Harber (1993) who studied peoples reactions after the Loma Prieta earthquake in California saw reactions to the incident change over different periods of time and stated "... just when a trauma becomes old news is when a second wave of adverse affects begin to crest."

It is important to understand the needs of survivors to distance themselves from the terror of their experience. Avoidance brings rest and renewed energy. Ironically once we begin to feel safe, any residual reactions not addressed or relieved initially may emerge once again.

If a return debriefing is offered, what is the optimum time needed to conduct this additional process?

No different: 1/2 hour - 2 hours.

Would the same process be used in a follow-up or additional sessions?

Yes, the same process is used. If this were a same day return, individuals may wish to return to a specific issue addressed in the earlier meeting. Each participant should be given the opportunity to share his thoughts and personal reactions to an issue.

If this is a continuation of an incomplete session, a brief review should be given before starting at the point where the process ended. If there is considerable time between sessions, from several weeks to a year, begin with a brief summary of the first meeting, ask if there are any questions and begin at the first stage by asking - "Are there any new or additional memories you have of what you saw, heard, etc. when this first happened or when you first found out?"

Can debriefing be provided to participants (professionals) who have been exposed to different trauma's at different times?

Yes. Regardless of the type of incident there are many shared common reactions to traumatic incidents whether violent or non-violent. The terror, fear, worry, hurt, guilt, anger are all quite common. Trauma-specific reactions such as intrusive thoughts, startle reactions, and physical symptoms are shared by most trauma victims.

Actually the debriefing process is an excellent model to use with professionals with varied experiences who might not otherwise receive debriefing on an individual basis. It helps to build a strong supportive network among professionals who realize the commonality of their experiences.

This "mixed" format is not common yet, when used with professionals with varied experiences, becomes a valuable learning experience for them as to the need to engage in regular debriefing sessions. Only skilled debriefers with clinical experience should conduct this process.

How many debriefers are needed?

Three debriefers are needed for groups of 8-10 participants. The first debriefer usually covers the introductory and fact finding stages, the second covers the personal reaction stages and the third covers the summary stage.

Debriefing can be done with two debriefers. However, if one of the participants should need to leave, a debriefer needs to accompany that person. This leaves only one person to debrief, a situation which should be avoided. The intensity of the material covered and the need to control the group process are best suited to at least three debriefers. The SITCAP model has three stages. One debriefer is used for each stage.

Who can be a debriefer?

Debriefers certainly need to be trained in the differences between grief and trauma for adults and children. They need to have some clinical experience in assessment and some group experience because of the format. With the use of three debriefers, one person can be new to the process, do well, and learn quickly with the support and feedback of the other two debriefers.

Some of the reasons schools and agencies have had difficulty in the past with debriefing experiences are that the debriefers were 1) trained in the "Mitchell Model" and unable to adapt this model to the school/agency setting 2) of a different profession and found it difficult to relate to educators and mental health workers or 3) not experienced working with children, adolescents and varied clinical populations, age and developmental differences.

Many school districts have moved to District Crisis Teams or Trauma Response Teams and use team members as debriefers. More mental health, child-family agencies and organizations are sending staff for debriefing training, to be better able to assist neighboring schools, staff within their own systems, and other community residents and businesses exposed to traumatic incidents.

Are there times or factors that might indicate a debriefer not debrief?

Yes. Vicarious traumatization is something all debriefers and trauma specialists must continually evaluate. Debriefing is difficult work and exposes debriefers and intervenors to the very reactions they attempt to help others overcome. The constant re-experiencing, intrusive thoughts, images, problems concentrating, staying focused, fatigue, problems controlling feelings, wishing you weren't a team member or responsible for debriefing are all indicators that you need to distance yourself until you can "reclaim" yourself. It is not advisable to be a debriefer in a situation in which you are familiar with the victim, such as a therapist, counselor, school administrator. You may think you can manage, but once in the group, find that it is too difficult to separate from your own feelings.

In addition, specific situations (incidents) may trigger strong emotional reactions that should preclude debriefing. These reactions will be experienced as you learn of the nature of the incident. This is why it is important to obtain incident information prior to initiating a session. When personal reactions are strong, it might be best to step back and let someone else conduct the debriefing.

At other times you simply may have just come out of a difficult situation and need a rest. Rather than be a direct debriefer, you may be more helpful taking on the role of operational debriefer for the debriefing which is less intrusive.

Are there ground rules?

Most definitely. Debriefing needs to be a very structured process. There is no way to know the emotional stability and well being of participants. Structure encourages the gradual release of those emotions which may otherwise become volatile or out of control. Turnbull (in Meichenbaum, 1994) wrote of his experiences debriefing relief workers following the Lockerbie air disaster:

"We also rapidly learned a cardinal rule in debriefing - that it is not advisable to begin with inquiring about the emotional reactions of 'exposure hardened' individuals. It was more effective (and easier) to collect together the overall experience of the group before exploring individual reactions."

Another reason debriefing needs to be a very structured process is because when in crisis, one needs structure and direction for stabilization - for slowing down the adrenaline, the out of control sense of powerlessness. Ground rules specific to the process provide this structure and direction.

Ground rules include: (complete detailing of rules and stages can be found in the Appendix)
- Only one person talks at a time
- If you cannot answer the question asked, you may pass and be returned to once others have responded
- There is no blaming, accusing
- There are to be no interruptions - phones and beepers are to be turned off
- Confidentiality is to be maintained, etc.

What about confidentiality?

Participants must be able to trust that their responses will be kept confidential. Often, during such intense sharing, participants may say more than they initially intended or hear things that are unexpected, even shocking.

Critical incident stress debriefing (CISD) is often used in response to incidents which involve law enforcement, investigators and those participants in the process of being questioned. This generates concern for confidentiality. As a result, it is recommended that notes not be taken.

A school-agency situation is likely to be much different and not involve participants who are involved with investigators. Note taking in this case can be reserved for the debriefer who will be completing the summary process. If notes will be taken to aide recall for the summary, it is important to inform participants prior to starting and ask if doing so creates a problem. Also, notify the group that the notes will be torn up at the end of the meeting so no written record will be available.

What do we do with those participants who have been told by police not to talk about details because of ongoing investigation?

Participants can pass on questions concerning details but can certainly respond to the majority of the questions posed by the different stages. The process can still be very beneficial as they listen to the reactions of others. It will help normalize reactions and let them be a part of a support group.

Should law enforcement representatives provide factual information to the group prior to starting the debriefing in cases where such details are available?

No. The value of the process is that each response helps to gradually develop the story, fill in details, correct misperceptions, and reveal new information. The process allows participants to listen to each other, integrate what they hear from one another into their own experience and reactions, and to come to the realization that what they share in common is not necessarily details but trauma-specific reactions themselves.

If participants have a need to have someone in authority provide factual information, do so by obtaining that information as a debriefer and then integrate it into the summary phase. Do not attempt to introduce factual information in the initial factual stage. This will change the focus of debriefing from being participant-generated to debriefer-generated. It will block participants' need to tell their story, which is critical to healing. Correcting false information and distorted perceptions is certainly critical but can be accomplished in the summary stage. If a classroom presentation occurred prior to debriefing, some of this information may have already been presented to those being debriefed.

Can debriefers be subpoenaed to testify about the information obtained during debriefing?

Yes. Just as anyone can be sued appropriately or inappropriately, anyone can be subpoenaed.

There is no need to keep records or notes of debriefing sessions. Without records it will be difficult to recall "who said what" much less "what" was said. Debriefing is so intense and covers so much that it will be very difficult to recall specifics. This is likely not to be an issue working with schools and agencies, but if it does occur, it is best to consult with an attorney.

When debriefing children, what additional concerns about confidentiality exist?

Children will talk. Maintaining confidentiality may be difficult. It probably is best to say to children something such as: "It is okay to talk to your friends and others about what it was like for you, but it is not okay to tell your friends or others what the others talked about."

What do we say to participants (adults) about phone calls, beepers, attending to students or other clients?

The rule is that phones and pagers are turned off during the session. Participants are not to be available to other staff or clients during debriefing. Interruptions are very detrimental to the value of the process and disruptive to other participants. The purpose of debriefing is to allow participants the time and attention needed to debrief. Being on call and accessible by phone, etc., prohibits this from being accomplished.

How should the room be set up?

Assuming that you accept the recommendations not to have more than 8-10 participants, the space needs to allow for all of you to sit in a circle or around a table. Sometimes a table acts as a "safe support". This is not a sensitivity group. The only purpose for sitting in a circle is for each member to be better able to listen to one another. It is best to have debriefers sit among participants in a gesture of support.

What props, refreshments do we need?

Kleenex is a must. With adults, coffee, pop, water, tea are okay. Once the group starts most will not be drinking. Beverages do sometimes act as a support - a comfort until the process begins. In some cases participants will have lunch or a snack. They may have been on the "front line" all day. Again, this is not psychotherapy. In trauma we need first to feel safe and protected before we can adequately face the experience. Let them eat or drink as they need unless it becomes very disruptive.

Children: Refreshments are not a good idea to have for children until after the session is completed. Children need as few distractions as possible during debriefing. It will be difficult enough for them to stay focused without adding refreshments.

What kind of handout material should be made available and when?

Handout materials are needed for adults. They can be provided prior to starting the session or presented following the session. Sometimes providing handouts just before people are getting settled gives participants something concrete to "hold onto" until the sessions begins. Handouts should provide information about 1) the nature of trauma and its reactions, 2) ways to take care of oneself when under stress, 3) what signs might indicate a need for additional assistance beyond debriefing, and 4) where to call for additional assistance if needed.

What procedure needs to be in place prior to debriefing to appropriately begin and end the session?

A supervisor/administrator must be identified and available on premise at all times for two reasons,

> 1) Occasionally a participant will find telling the story or listening to it emotionally overwhelming and will get up and leave. One of the debriefers will need to follow and provide crisis intervention as needed. The supervisor/administrator is legally liable for the staff person. If this person chooses not to return to the group, the supervisor/administrator must make the final decision about allowing the person to leave the premises. The debriefers can certainly consult with the administrator

regarding the staff person's status. It is critical, therefore, that the debriefers assigned to assist those who may leave be experienced in crisis intervention.

2) During the Summary Stage you will be asking participants what might be helpful for them during the next several days to best get through those days. Often in schools and agencies, participants will want time off, coverage for clients, etc. These will be requests only administrators can answer. It is appropriate to have a brief discussion with the administrator and ask him to meet with the group, to offer whatever resources or support possible. This can be done before the group ends. Although some decisions may not be immediately possible, just knowing that their requests will be considered and some response will be forthcoming can relieve some of their stress.

It is wise as a debriefer to inform the administrator prior to debriefing that staff may ask for some release time, additional help, or temporary change in duties.

Do debriefers have a script?

Yes. It is appropriate for each debriefer to have 5 x 7 index cards or a similar format that includes the questions of the assigned stage. It is appropriate to let participants know that you do have a list of the questions you will be asking to help keep you, the debriefer, focused on the process while also listening to the grief and horror of their experiences. It is very easy to become so involved that questions and comments committed to memory may be lost. The notes ensure that all the issues will be covered and that the debriefing process will be comprehensive and as beneficial as possible.

Can debriefers use their own words when asking the debriefing questions?

It is recommended that debriefers follow the script. The questions use specific words and phrases which direct themselves to specific trauma references. Experience teaches us that when given the flexibility to use ones own words, the focus is often lost, the value of externalizing specific trauma references is minimized, and debriefers tend to become less focused and slip into more traditional clinical interview processes.

Must debriefers always direct questions to participants in the same order?

Remember that a crisis brings terror and fear. Order and structure help reduce that fear and bring about stabilization. By moving around the circle of participants in the same order following each question, participants are given the opportunity to prepare their answer as well as listen to the answers being given as they know when their turn is coming and that the question will be repeated should they not be able to remember the question because of the intrusiveness of thoughts and images being experienced. There is safety and control in the process - the very two experiences victims of trauma struggle to reclaim.

Is it appropriate to ask multiple questions of participants at one time?

No. Again, in the state of crisis, simplicity and clarity are essential. These questions are designed to bring focus to specific trauma reactions. Multiple questions not only become confusing, but break down the structured process of asking one question of each participant, one at a time.

Trained counselors, social workers, and psychologists, when first learning how to debrief fall into old patterns of pursuing an issue with multiple questions. Debriefing is not therapy. The debriefing process is quite a different process than most have been trained to use.

When is it appropriate to ask for clarification, to reflect, to normalize?

This question again reflects the methodology so many professionals have been trained to use in individual and group interventions. Yes, there are times to normalize and reflect. However, experience has taught us that when done too early or too frequently it inhibits participants from telling their story.

This issue is similar to a child who is crying as he relates his painful experience. The "gut" reaction may be to give the youngster a hug to comfort him but in fact it would remove him from the pain he so desperately needs to face and externalize. Hugging, whether physically or verbally during the expressing of one's pain, shuts down the process at a point where it is important to "get it out" where it can more easily be resolved or controlled. Too much reflecting, normalizing too early creates the same result. Reflections, normalizations, even elaboration in our experience can be reserved for the summary stage.

If there are multiple victims involved with the incident being debriefed, how are participants asked about their relationship to and experience with the victims?

This can be managed by asking "Could you please tell us who you are and to which of the victims you are related? If you are not directly related to the victim, then tell us how you were involved with the incident."

What don't we want to ask initially?

Do not begin by asking participants how they are feeling. Remember, you may not have any idea how severely participants have been impacted. In a crisis state you want to lower anxiety not increase it. Asking about feelings can quickly and sometimes dangerously escalate reactions to the out-of-control level. In addition, debriefing is not therapy. It is not the purpose of the process nor your role as debriefer to probe feelings, but to simply identify, acknowledge and later normalize emotional reactions.

What do we ask about initially?

Relationships and facts. By asking participants to explain their relationship to the victim(s) and the details of their exposure to the incident, the focus is taken off the emotional intensity they may be experiencing and is placed into the cognitive realm. Sharing concrete information can lesson anxiety and more easily establish a sense of control.

Debriefing is not counseling. It is very structured. The purpose is not to interpret, analyze or process feelings, but to educate, normalize, prepare, and assist with identifying those resources and system changes needed to make the days following a critical incident a little easier. It is designed to address the major trauma reactions that can follow exposure to a critical incident - the fear, terror, worry, hurt, anger, revenge, accountability and survivor versus victim responses.

Debriefing may not benefit everyone. During the session some participants may, by their responses, indicate a need for additional intervention beyond debriefing. However, education about trauma and the normalization of reactions remain beneficial even for those who may need additional intervention.

The Five Models
School - Agency Based

Each model has specific purposes and is designed to meet the needs of a specific group such as students, staff in general, or crisis team members. Although the stages of each model are different, each model focuses on the major themes of trauma.

Debriefing

Purposes:
- to mitigate impact of event
- to accelerate healing
- to identify what happened
- to identify what role participants played
- to identify what cognitive behavioral & emotional reactions were experienced
- to educate about signs & symptoms
- to normalize
- to identify related issues, support needed
- to summarize and prepare for next several days, weeks, months
- to refer as needed

For Whom:
- reserved for most exposed students (5th - 6th grade and up) and staff

When:
- initiated three days to two weeks after event (even months later is appropriate)
- follow up debriefing 4-6 weeks after the incident

Size:
- limit to 8-10 participants per group

Conducted By:
- three debriefers (can be crisis team members)

Duration:
- two hours

Format:
- question, answer, inform

Debriefing Stages

Introductory Story Stage
This stage includes the introduction by the leader of the debriefers, the goals of debriefing, an orientation to its process, the ground rules, details of the participants' exposure to the incident and their cognitive reactions to it.

Personal Reaction Stage
This stage includes the sharing of physical and emotional reactions experienced at the time of the incident up to this point in the session.

Summary Stage
This stage includes a review of information shared, normalization of reactions, education as to what additional reactions and issues may yet emerge, identification of problems specific to the response of others and/or need for additional support and resources, review of ways to care for self inclusive of referral information.

Stage Assignment
Prior to beginning the session, one debriefer experienced in crisis intervention, must be assigned the role of following and intervening with any participant who leaves the session prematurely. A leader of the debriefing team must be determined and be responsible for consulting with the designated person administratively responsible for attending participants. The consultation involves site arrangements, participant back-up coverage, supporting non-access to participants, faculty response to participant requests for possible additional support and/or need for immediate resolution.

Defusing

Purposes:
- includes all the purposes of debriefing

For Whom:
- reserved for most exposed children K - 5th grade

When:
- initiated three days to one week after the event
- follow up 2-6 weeks after initial debriefing

Size:
- can be conducted with most exposed class (limit to 30 students)

Conducted By:
- two to four debriefers depending upon size of group and age

Duration:
- 30 minutes to one hour

Format:
- question, answer, inform, drawing, story telling, reading

What are the stages of defusing?

There are five defusing stages in the model:

Introduction - Information related to the incident is shared along with acknowledgement of the different ways they are feeling, what you will be doing to help them, and the ground rules they are to follow.

Generalization - In this phase, before asking about the specific incident itself, the nature of the incident is generalized and the children are asked to share who has had a friend or family member who has experienced a similar type of situation.

For example, a teacher is suddenly killed in an auto accident. Before asking or answering questions about the specific details of the teacher's death, the incident is generalized. The initial focus begins with their understanding of what an accident is and who in their family or someone they know has had an accident, what kind, etc. Examples of reflective summary statements for an accident can include: *Sometimes accidents only hurt people a little. Sometimes a lot. And sometimes people die in accidents (depending upon age level their understanding of death, its permanency, etc., will need to be explored). Sometimes other people cause accidents. Sometimes accidents happen because we are not paying attention, and sometimes accidents just happen, and no one is to blame.*

Specification - Once children have had the opportunity to share stories about their knowledge or experiences with the more generalized nature of the incident, they will be ready to move to the specific incident itself.

In this stage very brief details are provided and the children are asked several questions regarding what they have been told or have heard. This is followed by answering any questions they have about what happened to the victim(s).

Externalization - The first three stages could take 10 - 20 minutes to complete. Following the third stage, processing takes on the form of psychomotor activities designed to help children externalize their reactions and regain some sense of power over them. Drawing and story telling are used as an impetus for them to make us a witness to the experience as they know it internally but for which they may not have words.

In this process children will be asked to draw a picture of the event and tell a story about it. Additional trauma-specific questions will be asked to help them tell their story and externalize their reactions. They will be asked what the worst, hardest, scariest parts were for them. They will be asked what there biggest worry is now and to show how big their worry is at the time.

In this group process children learn that they are not alone with their fears and worries, that others are having or had the same reactions and that these are not unusual. They will experience some relief from their fear and worry and support from one another. Individually, it will take longer to see results because of the absence of the feedback and support from peers. Group participation is encouraged whenever possible.

Closure - This is the final stage. Cognitive reframing is accomplished via the summary and metaphorical reflections which the children are provided The major focus is on the meaning of becoming survivors. This is best accomplished through a brief summary and reflective statements (cognitive reframing).

Operational Debriefing

Purposes:
- to evaluate current status of staff and students/clients
- to share new information and clarify rumors
- to determine additional needs for immediate resources and support
- to prepare staff for possible upcoming problems

- to help staff care for themselves
- to reinforce positive aspects emerging from this event

For Whom:
- appropriate for entire staff

When:
- initiated first day
- follow up in three to five days, thereafter as determined by duration of event

Size:
- any number

Conducted By:
- outside consultant

Duration:
- one hour

Format:
- question, answer, inform

Student/Client Reactions:

To safely initiate staff feedback as to student/client reactions which dictate a response.

Staff Reactions:

To identify staff concerns related to system issues which did not help during the initial efforts to assist students.

Administrative Issues:

To identify what yet needs to happen and/or change to assist all involved, to answer questions of staff, and to identify the positive things that have happened.

Summary:

To educate staff about trauma reactions, normalize reactions and prepare them for reactions yet to come. To provide staff the opportunity to ask questions and support their overall effort to help students/clients.

Debriefing of Crisis Teams Members

Purposes:
- to help process difficult personal reactions
- to identify procedural systemic issues which helped or hindered effective interventions
- to evaluate each debriefers performance and overall team performance
- prepare for future debriefings

For Whom:
- crisis team members, debriefers

When:
- end of first day or as soon as possible after debriefing process

Size:
- limit to no more than 10

Conducted By:
- outside consultant

Duration:
- one to two hours

Format:
- question, answer, exploratory, problem solving

Debriefing Team Member Stages

Procedural Systemic Issues:

To identify the overall systems (administrative/management) responses which supported and/or impaired the teams ability to effectively intervene with the most exposed.

Personal Reactions:

To identify team members personal reactions which they were not prepared for and/or are struggling to overcome or adjust to.

Individual and Team Evaluation:

To identify areas of effectiveness and weaknesses in the overall team performance and individual performances to use as a learning experience to better prepare for future incidents.

Summary and Recommendations:
To review observations about systemic issues and recommendations to support and/or change; to normalize individual and team responses, vicarious traumatization, suggestions for self care and recommendations to improve and strengthen their level of preparedness and intervention responses.

Classroom Presentation

Purposes:
- to gather information on students' reactions, questions, concerns, information about event and victim(s)
- to provide factual information to minimize rumors, misperceptions
- to normalize current reactions
- to educate as to possible future reactions and what students can do and where they can go for help
- to identify appropriate behavior in the midst of such a crisis
- to encourage students to ask for help if needed/referral
- to inform of upcoming related activities e.g. memorial service

For Whom:
- appropriate for all grades

When:
- initiate immediately - within first week

Size:
- entire classroom participation

Conducted By:
- crisis team - one-two members or teachers and team member

Duration:
- 30 - 45 minutes
- one time presentation

Format:
- question, answer, inform, problem solve

Classroom Stages

Introduction:

To identify who you are, why you are there, what you are going to do and what you will be asking them to do.

Beginning:

To review the factual details of the incident to determine if others have heard anything different (rumors), to identify if anyone has been exposed to similar incidents in the past, and what upsets them the most about what happened.

Normalize:

To identify for them all the reactions they are likely to have that are specific to the nature of the incident - suicide versus homicide, versus accidental death, etc.

Identifying Appropriate Behavior:

To teach responsible behavior, caring behavior in the midst of a crisis as well as unacceptable behavior (primarily fighting, blaming).

Conclusion:

To provide the opportunity for students to ask questions, to inform them of what will be happening the rest of the day or next several days, to inform them how they can get help if they need to talk or find it difficult to manage their reactions, and to provide your own personal reactions (be honest) as a way of saying, "This is hard for all of us. We need to work through this together."

With the increasing number of critical incidents experienced by schools and child and family agencies, it is critical to have a response that addresses the unique needs of staff and students, staff and clients. These needs are different than rescue personnel exposed to community environmental catastrophic situations. Students especially look to and expect that their own teachers and counselors will be the ones to help them because they know them best. And the reality is very few people outside the school system understand or are effective in responding to the uniqueness of the school environment, the staff and student body. Crisis team members, therefore, need to be trained to conduct these specific models of debriefing as well as become aware of and skilled in managing process issues.

Final Considerations
At-Risk Participants

What are the issues related to potentially at-risk participants?

All survivors of a trauma-inducing incident are potentially at risk for chronic stress or posttraumatic stress. It is difficult to determine who may be at risk during that initial four week acute stress period due to delayed reactions and all the factors in the environment which prolong and/or induce delayed reactions. It is therefore recommended that following an initial debriefing period, a second session be scheduled sometime after the four week period. The purpose of this session is to better identify those survivors who are not coping well and may indeed be experiencing more severe reactions and symptomatology.

Assessment for potentially at risk individuals is complex. In disaster situations assessment is compounded by environmental factors, community response and resources available. Law enforcement, the judicial system and the media can all contribute to such factors for survivors. Solomon & Green (1992) propose that vulnerability to more severe reactions can be identified during three different periods: 0 to 3 months, 3 to 18 months and 18 months plus.

Meichenbaum (1994) reviewed numerous assessment tools and criteria of vulnerability. He identified 58 items and classified them under three headings: 1) Characteristics of the Disaster, 2) Characteristics of the Post Disaster, 3) Responses and Characteristics of the Individual and Group.

Most often schools and agencies request debriefing following incidents not directly threatening the lives of the entire community, such as suicide, overturned school bus, sudden death of student or staff person, shootings, or car fatalities. Occasionally debriefing is requested following community disasters such as floods, hurricanes, or terrorism.

Although disasters generate more potential for at-risk survivors than non-catastrophic incidents, each share common factors. Some factors placing survivors at risk are: proximity to the incident, the duration, exposure to grotesque death or critical injury, perception of a threat to life, the experience of powerlessness, somatic reactions, lack of support, exposure to continued stress, secondary victimization, and prior exposure to a traumatic incident. Exposure to these factors may necessitate additional follow up beyond the first four weeks.

Participants in the Summary Stage of debriefing need to be told the following - "Should the reactions you are experiencing now during the first four weeks continue anytime after the four week period it will be in your best interest to call us (or contact a trauma specialist). Again, it will not be unusual for these reactions to continue or emerge later. It takes time to recover from a trauma. The real concern is that if you do not get some assistance, these reactions may not only become chronic, but trigger additional problems for you. So please, do not hesitate to call us." (or contact a trauma specialist)

It is beneficial for staff from school and agency settings to be debriefed by trained debriefers from neighboring agencies versus debriefing by their own staff. It provides participants with a contact person they can call directly and in confidence should additional assistance be needed.

It is also beneficial to follow the initial debriefing with a follow up session anytime after the initial four weeks - for example, at three months, nine months, to one year (Williams et al. 1994) as a precaution against chronic reactions not previously addressed.

If a participant needs individual attention, what do we do?

Should a participant lose control and exhibit behaviors which are of concern but not life threatening, it is appropriate for a debriefer to recommend additional help to that individual before leaving him with the responsible administrator.

If the concern is for that individual's safety because of potential suicidal behavior, then the liability and choices are quite clear - you must inform the administrative supervisor of your concern preferably in the presence of the potentially suicidal individual and the responsible administrator. The school or agency's protocol for responding to potentially suicidal students or staff are then to be instituted by the administrative supervisor. You are responsible for making sure this happens. Failure to follow through on your part could be viewed as negligence. We recommend TLC's *Protocol Manual for Schools* (Steele, 2001) for schools who do not have protocol in place.

Additionally, should there be concern for a participant's ability to drive home or to return to operating vehicles or machines that could place that person or others at risk, you would also inform the administrator/supervisor to determine the most appropriate intervention.

Because debriefing is so structured and generally occurs three or more days after the incident, these concerns generally do not arise. Nevertheless, as a debriefer it is your responsibility to be prepared and to act responsibly.

Who is ultimately responsible for that person's safety?
There is no reason for one individual to carry the burden of determining what is best for an at-risk individual. This is the joint responsibility of the debriefers, administrators/supervisors and crisis teams.

As a debriefer, you are acting in the role of facilitator - not a clinician or intervention specialist. You are providing assistance, support and the opportunity for participants to talk about their experiences. Should concern for a participant arise, your role is to provide additional support and assistance by informing the responsible administrator. You may also need to do some immediate crisis intervention. Never make the final determination of what is best for the individual by yourself. Consult with the other debriefers and the administrator/supervisor.

Are there characteristics which distinguish victims from survivors?
Yes. Victims believe they are powerless to take control of their lives - that bad things have to be accepted because there is nothing that can be done about them. Victims do not feel they deserve to be cared for because they are flawed, inept, inadequate. Victims usually have little energy and often isolate themselves because they believe no one can be trusted and no one could possible understand the ordeal they have experienced.

Survivors become survivors as they take a direct active role in healing. They realize choices are always available and that despite their experiences they can always learn, improve, and create a better future with personal meaning. They realize there will be disappointments but that these too are manageable. They see themselves as deserving of love and support.

The major difference between victims and survivors is that survivors can reach out and accept help, whereas victims passively wait for help to come their way but when available can have a difficult time embracing help.

When do we make a referral for additional assistance?

Your ability to recognize a participant's need for additional assistance will be partly based upon intervention experiences with traumatized individuals and your understanding of "the risk to self or others" they pose.

It is imperative that you not only know the differences between grief and trauma but are able to recognize these through behavior, verbalization and responses to trauma-specific questions.

The debriefing process asks very trauma-specific questions. These questions are designed to provide information needed to build a picture of the kinds of stress reactions each participant is experiencing. The key issues become 1) can the individual function with some level of normalcy and 2) do they have an available support system? Realizing that you may initially be debriefing individuals during the acute stress stage, and that these reactions may not go beyond this period, you need to check back in several weeks to best determine the person's status at that time.

If a participant has a limited support system (one that is not willing to learn about trauma, listen to the victim, nor encourage the telling of their story, etc.), this person is likely to find recovery more difficult and needs to be encouraged after the initial debriefing to have a follow up visit.

The individual who is having difficulty returning to their level of functioning prior to the trauma four weeks beyond the acute stress stage is going to need additional intervention. Forgetting that one has something boiling on the stove, coming in late to work, unable to perform at a level prior to the trauma, difficulty concentrating, and difficulty completing tasks are all indicators that additional assistance is needed when continuing beyond that four week period.

The authors strongly encourage debriefing training. Debriefing is not counseling nor like counseling. Those who participate in the Institute's training initially find it very difficult to stay away from their traditional counseling skills. In initial role playing, experienced counselors turn debriefing into group counseling which intensifies anxiety. It does not reduce it. Safety is also the priority in debriefing. Taking a counseling approach does not lead to safety.

CHAPTER TEN
Intervention Questions, Answers and Anecdotal Accounts

Q. How soon after a trauma can SITCAP interventions be provided?

Acute Stress reactions as detailed in the DSM-IV appear from the onset of the incident up to four weeks following the incident. Reactions of Acute Stress are the same reactions of PTSD. The only difference between the two is a period of four weeks. When Acute Stress reactions continue beyond a four-week period following a traumatic incident, the diagnostic category becomes PTSD. These are very normal reactions during what can be called the initial recovery period. All too often these reactions cause grave concern because they are new and unusual for those not familiar with trauma. Is intervention helpful during this period? Yes, but not the more formalized structured intervention used for posttraumatic stress disorder (PTSD).

Victims of trauma do need assistance during these initial four weeks to accelerate the healing process and hopefully prevent movement into PTSD. During the first two days following a traumatic incident, shock and denial are often working overtime. What is needed, more than anything else, is information and direction as to what to do. In school settings this is accomplished by classroom presentations, which is part of the SITCAP debriefing component. Basic crisis intervention will also be needed for those most exposed. For people in the community, crisis intervention is provided often by county-wide crisis teams. Information is provided by those teams and/or the organizations involved. County critical incident stress management teams may provide some forms of debriefing the first few days.

On the third day, when shock and denial are less dominant, formal debriefing is provided to those most exposed. This process is helpful to most. However, some may have delayed reactions and not be included. Others may still be very emotional and physically overwhelmed and be unable to go through this cognitive process. These individuals are likely to need assistance at some future point. There are also some participants for whom debriefing triggers additional reactions.

With debriefing it is critical to return to those who participated in this initial debriefing, approximately six to eight weeks later. Some may move into PTSD. Others may not need additional intervention. The only way to really evaluate the status of the most exposed is to return to them at this later date.

In schools debriefing is also provided to staff. Operational Debriefing using the SITCAP model is provided to the entire staff at the end of the first day of the incident and thereafter every two to three days until major functions have returned to their previous pre-trauma level. The purpose of this type of debriefing, as detailed in Chapter Nine, is different than debriefing for the most exposed.

For those who may need additional intervention the use of SITCAP's eight-session intervention programs are recommended. This intervention can be provided six to eight weeks after the incident or years later. As detailed in the text, this intervention is far less cognitive than debriefing. It is, in fact, sensory based with cognitive reframing as the last component following exposure and trauma narrative intervention.

Regarding the four-week Acute Stress period, it is important to consider that this period can be prolonged when the trauma incident itself has prevented the return of the normal operating systems of one's infrastructure. This happens frequently in community tragedies when floods or hurricanes, for example, take out the main roads, electricity, and water. The absence of these day-to-day support systems can prolong and sometimes intensify the reactions of Acute Stress. A prolonged delay can also increase vulnerability to PTSD.

Q. How do we help an entire family who has been traumatized?

Although very time consuming, each member needs to be seen individually when an entire family has been traumatized. Each member needs the opportunity to tell his/her own story, as each member will be impacted differently. Once each member has gone through this individual process, the entire family can be seen together to tell their stories.

To meet with the entire family following a trauma is difficult. Members simply look at one another, and the memories of what happened are triggered. It is as if they can never get away from it. This explains why, in most cases, even in the most "open" of family systems, members will each take different roads in their attempt to get away from or get distance from the trauma experience.

The purpose of meeting with each individual member is to first recreate a sense of safety that allows each, in privacy, to relive the way he/she reacted, to develop their story (trauma narrative), and then reorder it (cognitive reframe) in a way they can now manage. Some may be able to accomplish this in one session; others may need several sessions. The SITCAP programs appropriate for each age level are used for this purpose. Sessions are followed sequentially. Not everyone will need every session. Once each member has found relief, and only after each member is feeling better, does the entire family sit down together to tell their stories to one another.

This family intervention generally takes no more than two hours and is initiated like a debriefing process. This too can be done weeks later, even years later. The point of meeting with each individual family member first is to help them get to a place where they feel safe enough to now relate to the other members of the family. Unfortunately when efforts are directed to trying to work with the entire family from the beginning, the family response is likely to be one of increased anxiety, of keeping "secrets" of how one reacted that may be triggering shame or guilt. This can be prevented in many cases by first meeting with each member individually.

Q. Do we ever see siblings together?

No, not initially. For the same reasons detailed in the answer to meeting with an entire family, meet with siblings separately. Children especially will have issues with safety. Each will want their own special attention. They certainly need to tell their own story, which they will be reluctant to do together. Embellishment, duplication, avoidance of different issues can be prevented by seeing siblings separately.

Q. What is the difference between individual and group intervention?

With the SITCAP model the only major difference is in the time. The activities, the focus on the sensations or themes remain the same. The group sessions are two hours in length versus the fifty-sixty minute sessions for individuals. It will simply take two hours for eight children to tell their story. It will take two hours for each to identify his/her biggest worry. Each "Session" addresses a major theme/sensation of trauma. Some children will have less reaction to worry than others; some will have more issues with hurt. It may therefore take one to two meetings to complete work on one session theme. For some it may take only twenty or thirty minutes to complete that session theme and then move on to the next theme. In field tests both individual and group interventions average eight meetings to complete all eight sessions.

The group format is actually much easier than the individual format. In the group program members normalize reactions for one another. Group members begin to support one another as "survivors". Not all people can tolerate the "stimuli" of group meetings. It can be overwhelming. The absence of privacy can also induce anxiety so that the individual program becomes safer.

It may not be realized that a child really needs the safety of individual intervention until several group sessions have been conducted. Safety is also the primary focal point throughout group intervention. For some, group intervention is safer than individual intervention. Whenever the safety of the individual is being or about to be jeopardized, intervention is directed to restoration of that sense of safety. For some it may mean the use of both individual and group; for others it may mean movement from individual to group, or group to individual.

Q. Is it important to follow the interventions in the sequence presented in the SITCAP Model?

Yes. Field testing and research has shown that some sensations are safer to manage than others. Each SITCAP session builds a sense of safety and power that then allows the engagement of the more difficult sensations such as anger and accountability. The outcomes documented in field testing and research are based upon following the intervention sequence.

Q. What if there have been multiple traumas, where do we begin?

Begin with the most recent trauma. Because SITCAP focuses on sensations rather than trauma related behaviors, multiple traumas to some degree become irrelevant in the intervention process. Hurt is hurt. The sensation of "hurt" will reflect the sensation of "hurt" experienced in multiple traumas.

This is not to say that there are not unique details to each experience that can play an important role in healing. These details may need to be pursued if intervening with the most recent trauma is not benefiting the client. It has been the Institute's experience, as reported by many of the two thousand certified consultants and specialists, that children do in fact experience relief without having to return to each and every trauma, because its themes cut across all types of incidents. These sensations are presented to the client, but the client defines the sensation. What hurt means to us is not necessarily what it means to the trauma victim. SITCAP allows the client to make us a witness to what that hurt was like or is still like. Letting the child tell us his story of "hurt" is what initiates the healing process.

Q. What if there is ongoing trauma?

Our Certified Consultants and Specialists have repeatedly reported that SITCAP intervention has given the children they work with a new resiliency, allowing them to direct their new energies to the other difficulties in their life. Becoming a survivor means not only to learn to negotiate one's present, threatening environment but to "know" they can survive future incidents. Any attention paid to empowering children in the midst of a threatening environment becomes one more link to the future; to a renewed sense of hope.

Q. What if a child's behavior suggests trauma, but there is no history available to validate trauma exposure?

Foster care children are placed in foster care because of some trauma. Confidentiality prohibits access to records. The Institute recommends dealing with the child in the present. As a starting point, we suggest beginning with "worry".

"Worry" is a safe place to begin with most children when there is no specific incident to identify. "Worry" then leads quite easily to addressing what has been the worst part of the present circumstances (being in foster care, school difficulties, etc.). The process then continues as directed in the SITCAP program.

Because we are again addressing sensations we can help the child gain relief even when facts of specific incidents are not available. Even if what the child is experiencing is not trauma, he/she still receives much needed help to deal with feelings in a way most never address. How many times do we actually spend time asking children about their biggest worry, how big it is, what it looks like, if it had a name what would be its name, what the child could do while he waits for the worry to go? "Worry" contains elements of fear and anxiety. Help a child with his "worry", even if it is not trauma related, and we help reduce his level of anxiety and fear. Reduce levels of anxiety and fear, and the child's ability to attend, focus, and be less reactive improves.

Q. Can trauma be experienced prior to age three?

If it is accepted that trauma is a sensory experience first, not a cognitive one, then there can be acceptance that children younger than three years of age do have a sensory memory of exposure to trauma. The October, 1999 Harvard Mental Health Letter (vol. 16, no. 4) reviewed research on the "Neurobiological Effects of Early Trauma." It discusses that early experience can cause prolonged hypersensitivity to Acute Stress.

People who suffer childhood trauma may suffer from persistent hyperactivity in the brain regions that contain CRF receptors. CRF (corticotrophin releasing factor) influences the immune system and autonomic nervous system. An increase in CRF can bring about reactions of depression and anxiety. Hyperactivity in the brain can result, which leaves individuals vulnerable to depression and posttraumatic stress disorder. This evidence strongly supports that trauma can impact a child's future prior to age three.

Although much more extensive, long-term research is needed, the Institute has been able to see decreases in arousal levels associated with mid-brain, trauma-triggered reactions. Because we deal with trauma at a sensory level, mid-brain arousal responses like hypervigilance can be reduced along with associated behavior. We also know that not all mid-brain responses can necessarily be altered by intervention alone. Medications can help reduce CRF secretions and associated reactions. The concept that is important to retain is that even in the absence of memory, the sensory impact of trauma can alter a child's response to life.

Q. How does trauma impact learning?

Dr. Bruce Perry (2000) reports that trauma "influences the pattern, intensity, and nature of sensory, perceptual and affective experience of events during childhood." Neurobiological changes induced by trauma are now related "to functional problems with memory and learning (the ability to attend, focus, retain, and recall) that accompany stress-related neuropsychiatric syndromes, including post-traumatic stress disorder."

Dr. Perry uses an example between two children with the same IQ, one exposed to trauma, the other not exposed. The one who is exposed to trauma is in the arousal (alarm) state. He "will be less efficient at processing and storing verbal information… cognition will be dominated by sub-cortical and limbic areas, focusing on non verbal information (the sensory level)- the teacher's facial expression, hand gestures." These children function better at the non-verbal level than the verbal level. And because of this arousal state, non-verbal cues are often read to be dangerous preludes to possible threat to self.

To help a traumatized child we must approach him first at the sensory level to attempt to decrease the arousal state, remove the threat and allow the brain to then function at the cognitive, verbal level. Once this is accomplished learning can begin or resume.

Q. Is there anyone who should not be included in SITCAP programs?

Caution is urged with those having a major psychiatric diagnostic disorder; Bipolar, paranoid schizophrenia, borderline personality. No research is available that identifies any population that should not engage in exposure-based intervention. We might say that those with major disorders are unable to exercise internal focus of control, and therefore sensory exposure may be too overwhelming. Depression and anxiety disorders can often benefit from such intervention, but any major disorder needs to be approached with caution.

In field tests the Institute worked with children diagnosed with autism, elective mutism, ADHD, depression, and a host of other disorders. Research is badly needed to isolate the unique trauma needs of special populations. There is still a great deal we do not know related to children. What we do know is that we must continue to challenge ourselves to seek out varied approaches to helping traumatized children.

Q. Is there a risk of re-traumatizing children by having them relive their experience?

If children do not feel safe, their response to intervention is likely to be "I have nothing to tell." If our only intervention is exposure which triggers a reaction- a sensory reliving, then risk does exist. The SITCAP model is very structured and guided by the priority on maintaining the safety of the child. Exposure is only the first step. We want to give that trauma a language, in a sense, to take it from a sensory memory and put it in a concrete tangible form, which can then be reordered or reworked in a way that the child's present life view of self and others becomes manageable.

Of the thousands of interventions being provided by Certified Consultants and Specialists across the country, we have not had one report since 1990 of any child unable to return to the classroom because he decompensated during SITCAP intervention. The intervention is a balance between dealing with trauma memories and pleasant memories. Because safety is always a priority, the activities inherently allow children to find their "safe place" should the activity become too difficult. This is supported and normalized. The child is empowered to determine what is safe.

All sessions are also moving the child from victim thinking to survivor thinking. Sessions move from the sensory to the cognitive as another way of returning to a "safe place." Sessions are structured to also end in a safe place. This is not to say that a child will not deteriorate. The belief is that if this were to happen, it would be because of the presence of other existing, comorbid disorders. Should decompensation begin, we support managing it no differently than if it were occurring when providing other forms of treatment.

Q. How is SITCAP intervention different from interventions provided by Protective Service agencies?

It has been the Institute's experience that child protective systems prohibit SITCAP intervention because these systems are often looking for at least initially, information to determine court-assigned issues with custody. This turns intervention into an investigatory process, which the child "knows" at a sensory level.

Many of our consultants return to tell about children "in the system." The SITCAP process is about becoming a witness to the child's experience. It is not about placing blame, finding fault, and gathering information to determine placement.

Consultants report their surprise at how cooperative, responsive, and relieved their children become when participating in SITCAP. Intervenors are there to be with the child in his terror, worry, hurt, anger, guilt, and powerlessness. The child "knows" this difference at a sensory level.

SITCAP is, in most child protective systems, in conflict with the assigned role of court workers and protective service workers. We in fact, over ten years, have had very little success integrating SITCAP into the "system." Still individual consultants in child protective agencies report the success they have had with children already "in the system." Later in this chapter a letter from one of the Institute's consultants describes how the Trauma Intervention Program for Children and Adolescents was challenged by the system. The outcome was positive.

There are, of course, systems that are open and working hard to change old line responses that offer minimal help. One such program in Ohio is the Children Who Witness Violence Program. The entire state has become invested in the program; the police, the court, prosecutors office, Attorney General, and agencies who make up the program. It is a wonderful effort that the Institute hopes is duplicated. Awareness related to children and trauma, how trauma manifests itself, and the trauma-specific intervention needs of children, remains relatively new information for many. Change based upon this new information about children and trauma will take time and a continued effort to educate those who have the influence to change the services of systems to meet the needs of today's children.

Q. Because drawing is a major component of SITCAP, what if the person doesn't want to draw?

If a child does not want to draw it may be that at a sensory level he doesn't feel safe. This has to be honored. On the other hand, the initial response to not wanting to draw is often in response to not knowing what to draw; not having a reference point. Because this is a very special circumstance, and because you have spent a good deal of time already educating and normalizing trauma as part of the SITCAP initial session, the child or adolescent has likely already given you some credibility, and trusts you to know what is best. Drawing still may be difficult. Following are suggestions to make the process a bit safer. Often children just need a reference point to start.

If they say,

"*I don't know how to draw.*"

Response – "*Oh sure you do. Even I do – not very good, but I can – here, let me show you.*" Draw one or two stick figures and then say, "*It doesn't matter how you draw, just that you draw.*"

"*I don't know what to draw.*"

Response – (Be patient) "*Well, think about what happened for a minute and then just start with any part of it you want.*" (Be patient and quiet. Give them time.)

"*I don't know how to draw it.*"

Response – "*What is it you are thinking about drawing?*" Have the child start out with just one part of the person, like a circle that will be the face. "*Why don't you just draw a circle and then the face.*" If it is an object, start with one part of the object i.e. car – "*Why don't you start with a square for the body of the car and then go from there.*"

"*I don't think this will help.*"

Response - "*I know. It seems strange, maybe even silly to you but believe me it will make everything that has happened a whole lot easier to handle. Remember the book...*" Pull out the book and reference the drawings of adolescents by saying, "*These are their drawings, and it did help. Let's give it a try and we'll see.*" If you have a few drawings of kids you have worked with and can speak personally about, use them. Use the most primitive drawings.

"*I don't want to do this.*"

Response – *"I know. Remember one of the reactions to trauma is not wanting to think about it or talk about it. It's hard. It brings up feelings you don't want, but the longer you avoid it the more power you give to those feelings to go on upsetting you."*

"I know it's hard even being here. It certainly isn't fair that this had to happen. It sucks. Maybe this is like going to a movie that scares you so much you can't sleep at night and you hear sounds in the house you never heard before and you get jumpy."

"Then, you go back and see the same movie over again maybe once or twice and what happens – it doesn't leave you scared anymore. That's what we're doing here. Helping you revisit what happened so you no longer have to be worried by whatever reactions you have because of it. So let's try. I'll ask you questions about what you're drawing to make it a bit easier. What do you want to start with in the drawing? We'll get that down and go from there."

IF HE REFUSES AT THIS POINT

Response – *"I know how difficult this can be, but I also know how helpful it can be. So maybe you can help me out with just one drawing. How about drawing me a picture of the person who died, was killed, injured, etc.?"*

If there is a "NO" response after all your efforts:

Response – *"Tell you what. Over the next couple of days why don't you just think about it and see if you can draw some aspect of what happened while you're at home and bring it in with you next time we meet. I usually don't pursue things this hard, but I know it can make a big difference. If you can't, I want you to know I'm okay with it because I do know that a trauma is like no other experience and most people wouldn't understand, but I do. It will be okay with me if drawing is something you don't want to do."*

At this point you would use trauma questions to help him tell his story. Most traumatized children and adolescents with gentle encouraging, following their first few responses, will engage in drawing. Once engaged, the use of the trauma-specific questions that follow will help them focus and begin to freely tell you their story.

Q. What happens once the drawing begins?

The trauma-specific process now begins. Once the child begins drawing about the incident itself, be curious about every aspect of the drawing. Ask questions about the different aspects, i.e., "What is this line?" Your curiosity encourages the continued release of trauma material and helps engage him in the process.

If he draws small faces, ask him to draw the same face larger and on another sheet of paper so you can see it more clearly. If he does not include himself in the drawing, ask him where he is and have him draw himself. Ask if there is anyone else not in the drawing, and, if so, ask him to draw and tell you about the person. As his story unfolds, you'll begin to develop a more comprehensive picture of the severity of his experience, his reactions to it, and his coping skills.

Some teens need to avoid the painful memories and will change the actual details or outcome of the event. Others will focus specifically on one aspect of their reaction and continue repetitive themes related to that response, such as the fear of what might happen to them in the future. Using trauma-specific questions helps you and the child remain focused on the incidents. The questions refer specifically to the incident and the child's reactions to it. They take you and the child through the range of possible PTSD reactions.

About Interpretation...

The use of drawing in this process is not to assess or interpret possible clinical diagnostic material. The use of drawing is a psychomotor activity designed to "stimulate" the senses in order to energize those trauma memories stored in the senses. Trauma is what we experience, not what we understand. The experience of trauma is largely a sensory experience, especially for children.

The interpretation of drawings takes years of experience. We do not recommend it. It benefits neither the child nor you, the intervenor. Attempting interpretations can lead you far astray and be detrimental to the child's healing. Your function in this drawing process is to encourage the child to draw about his experience and tell his story. In the process, he finds relief from his terror while bringing you into the experience as a witness, so he is no longer alone with his fear. It is a process that encourages a renewed sense of inner control and empowerment. Simply being curious and inquisitive about what he draws provides the vehicle and opportunity he needs to diminish the power of those terrifying sensory memories and replace them with more positive pleasurable memories.

One Last Comment

If children cannot draw, after providing these options, the Institute directs Consultants and Specialists to support the child's need for safety, to normalize how difficult reliving can be even for adults. This leaves us with a strictly cognitive approach. The child is asked to tell his story with the help of trauma-specific questions related to the details of the incident but also the sensations likely experienced. Once the story is told, cognitive reframing is used to help reorder the experience. If this is not possible, writing a journal, play therapy, attending to the child the best way possible at the time can still be beneficial. What we do not want to do is abandon the child, to leave him to struggle alone with his trauma- a victory which is all but impossible for a child.

Q. What if the child doesn't want to talk?

The response "I don't want to talk about it," can be the result of three situations. Situation one refers to the child's experiences with trying to talk about the details to his parents or other adults. The details terrify the adult. Predictably the adult says, "This is only making us feel worse. It's not helping. It's best we stop talking about it and get on with things." This is an understandable response as exposure via details can be frightening and leave the adult frightened that they and the child will lose control over this experience. The child is then left believing that adults really do not want to hear the details, so he says "No" to those who ask him to talk about it.

Situation two relates to not having words to adequately describe the experience. Even adults will have a difficult time finding words to describe their experiences. So when the child is asked if he wants to talk about it, he may want to but becomes anxious because he doesn't have the words and then shuts down.

Situation three is related to a psychological response that is similar to stuttering. For some it is almost impossible to form the words. It's as if they get stuck in the throat and the vocal cords can't "push" them out. This response to talking about what would terrify anyone can easily lead to a not wanting to talk about what happened. Safety again becomes critical to making this less frightening. Drawing is a way to safely communicate what a child may not have words to adequately describe.

Q. What if a parent is not agreeable to taking part in being a witness during the parent-child session?

Without parental involvement, the level of reduction of reactions and severity levels is likely to be less than if the parent was involved. Research detailing the importance of parental involvement was detailed in earlier chapters.

If using the group program one of the other parents could "adopt" the parentless child. The child could be assigned a special task that assists you so he experiences a connectedness to you. The abandonment by the parent will make it difficult. This is a child that, if possible, you will want to have a long term relationship with until the child can make other adult connections.

Q. Are there activities other than drawing that can help trauma victims?

Yes. However the Institute recommends its initial structured intervention because it is designed for safety, it moves very slowly and helps to isolate the major troublesome areas very quickly so, should additional intervention be needed, it has an immediate focus. Other methods can certainly be helpful. However, other interventions tend to lack structure, which lessens the sense of safety. They tend to be directed by the "insight" or analysis of the intervenor as to what the child needs, versus letting the child identify how he was impacted and what he needs.

The Institute believes that initial trauma intervention efforts need to have a very structured beginning and a very structured ending. This assists in making the intervention a positive one the child can safely manage and be willing to return to at a later time if needed. When we let the child direct us, he can re-experience a sense of empowerment and positive relationship to intervention. After all, the trauma is the child's experience, not the intervenor's experience. The child knows, if given the opportunity at a sensory level, what can help him feel better.

Anecdotal Responses

One of the unique values of SITCAP is its adaptability in both school and agency settings by varied professional disciplines working with varied populations and an array of violent and non-assaultive induced traumas. Following are several letters sent to the Institute by those who used one or more of the SITCAP intervention programs.

May, 1998
Dear TLC,

"I am writing this letter to share my experience with TLC's *Trauma Intervention Program*. I am a clinical psychologist and have used, and continue to use, many of the TLC intervention programs."

"I was working with a nine-year-old youngster who was referred for trauma associated with sexual abuse. Without thoughts or worries about a possible court trial, I immediately pulled out my trauma response materials. After approximately nine months this case went to trial. The defense attorney worked at saying we asked leading questions, planted memories, and attempted to build a case on false memory syndrome. However, upon seeing the trauma workbook the defense was not able to 'pull' out anything that could be damaging to the case. The defense struggled to find any leading questions and/or any way I had implemented these memories with the youngster."

"In closing, I am sending a BIG thank you to the team who created the intervention workbooks. The trauma workbook was solid and unable to be torn apart on the witness stand. Thank you for creating such a practical tool. As a clinician, I know this workbook can help families manage trauma. I have also learned that this workbook holds up strong in a court system that sometimes struggles to see and understand trauma."

Sincerely,
Julie MacArthur, Clinical Psychologist
Shelby Family Care Center
Shelby, Michigan

July 1, 1998
Dear TLC,

"I have been intending to write for some time, but have been incredibly busy ever since returning from the TLC Summer Institute in July 2000. At the time I completed my certification as a Trauma and Loss Consultant and School Specialist."

"As a parish minister I have often been called to area schools when a student death occurred. This happened again just two weeks ago. The difference was that this time I really felt like I had something significant and healing to offer the students and staff I interacted with. *Trauma Debriefing for Schools and Agencies* gave me the tools I needed to be of real help to high school juniors in a small rural school."

"I am learning a tremendous amount about caring for myself as well, in the midst of this work. Not surprisingly, I have needed to revisit some of my own childhood traumas. I am extremely grateful for the colleague who is assisting me in this personal work and encourage you never to let up on the vital importance of self-care and professional debriefing."

"My dream and my passion is to help youngsters learn that whatever painful experiences they go through they possess the courage and strength to gain wisdom from the experience and move forward in this grand adventure we call life. Thank you, for giving me the tools I need to see that dream become a reality."

Rev. Robyn J. Plocher, Director
Rick's House of Hope, Davenport, Iowa

October, 2000
Dear TLC,

"I am a licensed school counselor and mental health counselor. I received my TLC Certification last spring as a School Specialist and Consultant. Since then I have had the opportunity to use the *I Feel Better Now!* group intervention. I found the materials and format to be invaluable in helping children communicate feelings and thoughts that previously were locked inside. This material was particularly useful for a group of young boys whose dads' had committed suicide. I have worked with troubled children for 12 years and as a rule incorporate drawings in my work with kids. I have always found this to be extremely therapeutic as a non-threatening vehicle of expression, perhaps that is why I was drawn to TLC's approach as it so easily complemented my own style."

"Recently I had my first experience conducting a debriefing for a group. It consisted of 10 teenage girls from an area school who had a close friend die in a car accident. This was without a doubt one of the most meaningful human experiences I have ever had the good fortune to be a part of. I can't thank you enough for the Trauma Debriefing training that made this experience possible. I could see the anxiety drain from their faces, hear thoughts and feelings expressed that they had been too ashamed, guilty, or scared to speak about to anyone. They were overwhelmingly grateful to me for the opportunity to talk so candidly about their innermost fears and feelings. I was touched and humbled by their strength and courage and felt privileged to be a part of their healing process."

Dennie Ohrazda, MS, LMHC
Elkhart, IN

October, 2000

Dear TLC,

"A few weeks ago (September, 2000) I began to work with a young foster child who presented with oppositional behavior at home and at school. She had temper tantrums and would rage when her biological mother's name was mentioned. This child has had multiple traumas such as abandonment, physical abuse and neglect, witness to an execution-type murder and possible sexual abuse. She had been in and out of 3 different foster homes before she was age six."

"I decided to use the TLC program, *What Color Is Your Hurt?* with this child. At first she wanted no part of the program and was in no way cooperative during weekly sessions. She would not talk about any traumas that she had experienced. We continued with the program anyway and now she looks forward to the sessions. Her teacher and relatives have mentioned that this child is calmer, is not rageful and displays only a few oppositional traits. Her adoptive parents have stated, 'She is not the same child that came to us several months ago.' They were delighted with her progress."

"I believe that the structured and playful sessions of the *What Color Is Your Hurt?* program has helped this child immensely. This child will continue to need some therapy to deal with her own individual issues, however, since going through this program, she is no longer alone with her trauma and has some context in which to place it. It is because of TLC that she has had this success."

Thanks,
Lynn K. Hunt, ACSW, DCSW
Clinical Social Worker,
CMHS of Livingston County, MI.

This article appeared in the Bellflower Center for Prevention of Child Abuse in Cuyahoga County, Ohio in the fall of 1999. The article *"Helping Children Who Witness Violence,"* describes the value of TLC's pre-school trauma intervention program, *What Color Is Your Hurt?* The Bellflower Center is part of an Ohio statewide program, Children Who Witness Violence.

"Sarah, age 4, draws a picture of her family for the Bellflower Center social worker who is visiting her house. Carefully, she uses crayons to describe what happened in her house on the night the police came. Sarah' artwork shows her mother with a black eye and two hands around her neck. Sarah tells the visitor that one hand is a man choking her mother, and the other hand is God protecting her mother from getting hurt."

Bellflower Center is one of the agencies providing ongoing social work services after initial intervention is performed by Mental Health Services. Social worker Laurie Garrett, Bellflower Center's, Children Who Witness Violence Program specialist, works primarily with families of children ages birth-6 years.

Garrett helps families address urgent issues and works directly with the children in their home or other safe location. Using *What Color Is Your Hurt?* designed by The National Institute for Trauma and Loss in Children. Garrett engages the children in drawing activities to help them describe the incidents that took place and how they were affected. Like Sarah in the story above, many of the children that Garrett sees have breakthroughs with the coloring activity, which she believes is an extremely effective method for helping young children who do not have sufficient verbal skills to convey their impressions of the violent events.

Because of the chaos that is often present in these family situations, it is hard to predict how the children will react to Garrett's visits. But for one little girl, Garrett knows that her work has made a difference.

"She used to have nightmares, so we would draw a picture of her dream and put it away," Garrett said. "Now she says, 'Laurie, I don't have nightmares anymore. When I have them, I draw pictures and put them away and I'm not scared."

Final Comment

The value of The National Institute for Trauma and Loss in Children is suggested by the two thousand professionals who have been certified and are not only using the SITCAP model of intervention but continuously updating the Institute as to outcomes, recommendations for research, continued study, and development of intervention activities and ongoing training. Certification training remains available through the Institute. As stated in the introduction, training allows one to "know" the process at a level that a cognitive approach cannot reach.

Contact TLC

For more information on the SITCAP model, the intervention programs or the TLC Trauma and Loss Certification Program or for the *Brave Bart* storybook or any other of the TLC books and videos you can contact TLC at:

TLC
The National Institute for Trauma and Loss in Children
900 Cook Road
Grosse Pointe Woods, Michigan 48236
(313) 885-0390 or toll-free at (877) 306-5256
email: steele@tlcinst.org
www.tlcinstitute.org

BIBLIOGRAPHY

Abbenante, J. (1982). <u>Art Therapy with Victims of Rape</u>. In A. DiMaria, E.S., Kramer, & E.roth (Eds.), Art Therapy: Still Growing, Proceedings of the 13th Annual Conference of the American Art Therapy Association (pp. 34-38) Baltimore, MD: AATA

American Psychiatric Association. (1994). <u>Diagnostic and Statistical Manual of Mental Disorders (DSM-IV)</u> (4th ed.). Washington, D.C.

American Psychiatric Association. (1980). <u>Diagnostic and Statistical Manual of Mental Disorders (DSM-III)</u> (3rd ed.). Washington, D.C.

American Psychiatric Association. (1968). <u>Diagnostic and Statistical Manual of Mental Disorders (DSM-II)</u> (2nd ed.). Washington, D.C.

American Psychiatric Association. (1952). <u>Diagnostic and Statistical Manual of Mental Disorders (DSM-I)</u> (1st ed.). Washington, D.C.

Beck, A.T. (1972). <u>Depression: Causes and Treatment</u>. Philadelphia: University of Philadelphia Press.

Beck, A.T. (1976). <u>Cognitive Therapy and the Emotional Disorders</u>. New York: International University Press.

Belenky, G. (Ed.) (1987). <u>Contemporary Studies in Combat Psychiatry</u>. New York: Greenwood Press.

Beyers, J. (1996). *Children of the stones: Art therapy interventions in the west bank.* <u>Art Therapy: Journal of the American Art Therapy Association</u> 13, 238-243.

Black, D., Hendricks, J. Kaplan, T. (1992). *Father kills mother: Post-traumatic stress disorder in children.* Psychotherapy Psychosom, 57, 152-157.

Bloch, D., Silber, E., Perry, S. (1956). *Some factors in the emotional reaction of children to disaster.* American Journal of Psychiatry, 112, 481-488.

Bradburn, I.S. (1991). *After the earth shook: Children's stress symptoms 6-8 Months After a Disaster.* Advances in Behavior Research Therapy, 13, 173-179.

Bradner, T. (1943). *Psychiatric observations among Finnish children during the Russian-Finish war of 1939-1940. Nervous child,* 2, 313-319. In, P.A. Saigh, J.D. Bremner, (1999) Posttraumatic Stress Disorder, Massachusetts, (p. 15)

Bremmer, J.D., Randall, P., Scott, T.M., Bronen, R.A., Seibyl, T.P., et al. (1995). *MRI-based measures of hippocampal volume in patients with PTSD.* American Journal of Psychiatry, 152, 973-981.

Cooper, N.A. Clum, G.A. (1989). *Imaginal flooding as a supplementary treatment for PTSD in combat veterans: A controlled study.* Behavior Therapy. 31, 381-391

Deblinger, E., Lippman, J. & Steer, R. (1996). *Sexually sbused children suffering posttraumatic stress symptoms: Initial treatment outcome Findings.* Child Maltreatment 1,310-321.

Dykman R., McPhearson, B., Ackerman, P., et al (1997). *Internalizing and externalizing characteristic of sexually and/or physically abused children.* Integrative Physiological and Behavioral Science 32, 62-74.

Emery P. (1996). *The inner world in the outer world: The phenomenology of posttraumatic stress disorder from a psychoanalytic perspective.* Journal of the American Academy of Psychoanalysis, 24(2) 273-291.

Ericksen, J.E. (1860). On Railway and Other Injuries of the Nervous System. Philadelphia: Henry C. Lea.

Eth, S. & Pynoos, R. (Eds). (1985). Post-traumatic Stress Disorder in Children. Washington, D.C. American Psychiatric Press.

Eth, S. & Pynoos, R. (1994). *Children who witness the homicide of a parent.* Psychiatry, 574 (4), 287.

Famularo, R., Kinscherff, R. & Fenton, T. (1992). *Psychiatric diagnosis of maltreated children: Preliminary findings.* Journal of American Academy of Child and Adolescent Psychiatry 31, 863-867.

Foa, E.B. Dancu, E., Hembree, E., Jaycox, L.H., & Meadows, E.A., (1997). Efficacy of Prolonged Exposure and Stress Inoculation Training for Chronic PTSD. (publisher unknown).

Foa, E.B. & Kozak, M.J. (1985). *Treatment of anxiety disorders: Implications for psychopathology.* In A.H. Tuma & J.D. Maser (Eds.), Anxiety and disorders. Hillsdale, NJ: Erlbaum.

Frank, E., Anderson, B., Stewart, B.D., Dancu, C., Hughes, C., & West, D. (1988). *Efficacy of cognitive behavior therapy and systematic desensitization in the treatment of rape trauma.* Behavior Therapy, 19, 403-420.

Frankl, V. (1960). Psychology and Psychiatry of the Concentration Camps. *In J. Kinzie, R. Goetz, (1996). A century of controversy surrounding posttraumatic stress-spectrum syndromes: The impact on DSM-III and DSM-IV.* Journal of Traumatic Stress 9. (2)169

Frederick, C.J., Pynoos, R., & Nader, K. (1992). Child Posttraumatic Stress Reaction Index. Unpublished Instrument.

Freud, S. (1959). *The aetiology of hysteria.* In J. Riviera (Trans.) Sigmund Freud: Collected Papers (Vol.1, pp 183-219). New York: Basic. (Original work published in 1856)

Garbarino, J. (1992). Children in Danger: Coping with the Consequences of Community Violence. CA. Josey-Bass Social and Behavioral Science Series and the Josey-Bass Education Series.

Golub, D. (1985). *Symbolic expression in posttraumatic stress disorder: Vietnam combat veterans in art therapy.* The Arts in Psychotherapy, 12, 285-296.

Grill, D. (1999). Deactivation. (in publication). Treatment Center for Traumatic Life Experiences, Brentwood, CA.

Herl, T. (1992). *Finding the light at the end of the tunnel: Working with child survivors of the Andover tornado.* Art Therapy: Journal of the American Art Therapy Association, 9 (1) 42-47.

Herman, J. (1992). Trauma and Recovery. New York, Basic Books.

Johnson, D. (1987). *The role of creative art therapies in the diagnosis and treatment of psychological training.* The Arts in Psychotherapy, 14, 7-13.

Johnson, K. (1993). School Crisis Management: A Hands-On Guide to Training Crisis Response Teams. Alameda, CA, Hunter House, Inc

Keane, T.M., Fairbank, J.A., Caddell, J.M. & Zimering, R.T. (1989). *Implosive (flooding) therapy reduces symptoms of PTSD in vietnam combat veterans.* Behavior Therapy, 20, 245-260.

Kinzie, D., Goetz, R. (1996). *A century of controversy surrounding posttraumatic stress-spectrum syndromes: The impact on DSM-III and DSM-IV.* Journal of Traumatic Stress, 9 (2).

Koplewicz, H.S., Vogel, J.M., Solanto, M.V. Morrissey, R.G., Alonzo, C.M., Gallagher, R., Abekoff, H.B., & Novich, R.M. (1994, October). *Child and parent response to world trade center bombing.* Poster presented at the Annual Meeting of the American Academy of Child and Adolescent Psychiatry, New York.

LaGreca, A.M., Silverman, W.K., Vernber, E.M. & Prinstein, M.J. (1996). *Symptoms of posttraumatic stress in children after hurricane Andrew: A prospective study.* Journal of Consulting and Clinical Psychology, 64, 712-723.

Lang, P.J., (1979). *A bio-informational theory of emotional imagery.* Psychophysiology, 16, 495-512.

LeDoux, I.E., Romanski, L., & Xagoraris, A., (1991). *Indelibility of subcortical emotional memories.* Journal of Cognitive Neuroscience, 1, 238-243,

Lonnigan, C., Shannon, M.., Finch., Daugherty, T., & Taylor, C. (1991). *Children's reactions to a natural disaster: Symptom severity and degree of exposure.* Advances in Behavior Research and Therapy 13, 135-154.

Malchiodi, C.(1998). Understanding Children's Drawings. New York, Guilford Publishing Co.

Malleson N. (1959). Panic and Phobia: A Possible Method of Treatment. Lancet, 1, 225-227.

March, J. Amaya-Jackson, L., Costanzo, P., Terry, R. & The Hamlet Fire Consortium. *Posttraumatic stress in children and adolescents after an industrial fire.* Selected Abstracts PTSD Research Quarterly, Fall, (1993, January). Paper presented at the Lake George Conference on PTSD

Matsakis, A. (1992). I Can't Get Over It: A Handbook for Trauma Survivors. Oakland, CA. New Harbinger Publications.

Matsakis, A., (1994). Posttraumatic Stress Disorder, New Harbinger Publications, Inc., CA

Marks, I.A. (1972). *Flooding (implosion) and allied treatments.* In S. Argas (Ed.) Behavior Modification: Principles and Clinical Applications (151-211) MA, Little Brown, & Co.

McFarlane, A.C. (1994). *Helping victims of disasters.* In J.R. Freedy & S.E. Hobfoll (Eds.). Traumatic Stress: From theory to practice. New York, Plenum.

McFarlane, A. C. (1988). *Recent life events and psychiatric disorder in children: The interaction with preceding extreme adversity.* Journal of Clinical Psychiatry, 29 (5), 677-690.

McFarlane, A., Policansky, S., & Irwin, C. (1987). *A longitudinal study of the psychological morbidity in children due to a natural disaster.* Psychological Medicine 17, 727-738.

Meichenbaum, D. (1994). A Clinical Handbook/Practical Therapist Manual For Assessing and Treating Adults with Post-Traumatic Stress Disorder (PTSD). Waterloo, Ontario, Canada, Institute Press.

Meichenbaum, D. (1974). *Self-instructional methods.* In F.H. Kanfer & A.P. Goldstein (Eds.) Helping People Change (pp. 357-391). New York: Pergamon Press.

Mihaescu, G., Baettig, D. (1996). An Integrated Model of Posttraumatic Stress Disorder. Eur. J. Psychiat. 10 (4), 243-245.

Milgram, N. Toubiana, Y., Klingman, A., Raviv, A., & Goldstein, I.(1988). *Situational exposure and personal loss in children's scute and chronic dtress reactions to a school bus disaster.* Journal of Traumatic Stress. 1, 339-351.

Mower, O.A. (1960). Learning Theory and Behavior. New York, Wiley

Perry, B. (2000). *Violence and childhood: How persisting fear can alter the developing child's brain.* The Child Trauma Academy. childtrauma@bcm.tmc.edu.

Peterson, S., & Straub, R. (1992). School Crisis Survival Guide. New York, The Center for Applied Research in Education.

Piers, C. *A return to the source: Rereading freud in the midst of contemporary trauma theory.* Psychotherapy. 33/Winter 1996, 540- 547.

Pynoos, R.S. (1994). Traumatic Stress and Developmental Psychopathology in Children and Adolescents. Sidran Press, Lutherville, MD, 171, 65-98.

Pynoos, R. & Eth, S. (1986). *Witness to violence: The child interview.* Journal of the American Academy of Child Psychiatry. 25, 306-319.

Pynoos, R., Nader, K., Arroyo, E., Steinberg., A., Eth, S., Nunez, F. & Fairbanks, L. (1987). *Life threat and posttraumatic stress in school age children.* Archives General Psychiatry 44, 1057-1063.

Pynoos, R., & Nader, K. (1988). *Psychological first aid and treatment approach to children exposed to community violence: Research implications.* Journal of Traumatic Stress 1, 445-473.

Pynoos, R., & Nader, K. (1990). *Children exposed to Violence and traumatic death.* Psychiatric Annals 20, 334-344.

Quarentilli, E. L. (1985). *Assessment of conflicting values of mental health: The consequence of traumatic events.* In C.R. Figley (Ed.) Trauma and Its Wake (pp. 173-218) New York, Brunner/Mazel.

Rachman, S.J. (1966). *Studies in desensitization-II: Flooding.* Behavior Research and Therapy. 4, 1-6.

Raider, M., Steele & W. Santiago, A. (1999). Trauma Response Kit: Short Term Trauma Intervention Model Evaluation. unpublished manuscript, Wayne State University, MI.

Riley, S. (1997). *Children's art and narratives: An opportunity to enhance therapy and a supervisory challenge.* The Supervision Bulletin, 9 (3), 2-3.

Roje, J. (1995). *LA '94 Earthquake in the eyes of children: Art therapy with elementary school children who were victims of disaster.* Art Therapy Journal of the American Art Therapy Association 12, 237-243.

Saigh, P.A. (1991). *On the development of posttraumatic stress disorder pursuant to different modes of traumatization.* Behavior Research and Therapy. 29, 213-216.

Saigh, P., (1987). *Invivo flooding of a childhood post-traumatic stress disorder.* School Psychology Review 16, 203-2211.

Saigh, P., Bremner, J. (1999). Posttraumatic Stress Disorder. Massachusetts

Schwarz, E. & Kowalski, J. (1991). *Posttraumatic stress disorder after a school shooting: Effects of symptom threshold selection and diagnosis by DSM-III-R, or Proposed DSM-IV.* American Journal of Psychiatry 48, 592-597.

Schwarzwald, J., Weisenber, M., Waysman, M., Solomon, Z., (1994). *Stress reaction of school age children to the bombardment by SCUD missiles: A 1-year follow-up.* Journal of Traumatic Stress, 7, 657-667.

Shaw, J. (1995). *Psychological effects of hurricane Andrew on elementary school population.* Journal of the Academy of Child and Adolescent Psychiatry. 34 (9), 1185-1192.

Shalev, A. (1994). *Debriefing following traumatic exposure.* In R.J. Ursano et al (Eds.) Trauma and Disaster. Cambridge: Cambridge University Press.

Shalev, A., Ursano, R. (1990). *Group debriefing following exposure to traumatic stress.* In B.A. van der Kolk, A. Mc Farlane, L. Weisaeth (Eds.) Traumatic Stress Disorder, (p. 59). New York, The Guilford Press, 59.

Stampfl, T.G., (1961). *Implosive therapy a learning theory derived psychodynamic technique.* Unpublished manuscript, John Carroll, University of Cleveland. In P.A. Saigh, J.D. Bremner. (1999) Posttraumatic Stress Disorder, (p. 354) Massachusetts.

Steele, W., (1999). Trauma Debriefing Handbook. TLC Institute, Grosse Pointe Woods, MI

Steele, W., (1992). Trauma Response Teams in Schools. TLC Institute, Grosse Pointe Woods, MI.

Steele, W., Raider, M., (1999). Intervention with Traumatized Children. Skillman Center for Children, College of Urban, Labor and Metropolitan Affairs, Wayne State University, Detroit, MI. Occasional Paper Series 2000, No.1. August 2000.

Stubner, M., Nader, K., Yasuda, P., Pynoos, R. & Cohen, S. (1991). *Stress responses after pediatric bone-marrow transplantation: Preliminary results of a prospective longitudinal study.* Journal of the American Academy of Child and Adolescent Psychiatry. 30, 952-957.

Terr, L. (1981). *Psychic trauma in children: Observations following the Chowchilla school bus kidnapping.* American Journal of Psychiatry 138, 14-19.

Terr, L. (1985). *Children traumatized in small groups.* In S. Eth & R. Pynoos (Eds.), Posttraumatic Stress Disorder in Children (pp 45-70). Washington: American Psychiatric Association.

Terr, L. (1990). Too Scared to Cry: Psychic Trauma in Childhood. New York: Harper and Row.

Terr, L. (1991). Childhood Traumas - An Outline and Overview. American Journal of Psychiatry. 148, 10-20.

Thompson, J.A., Charlton, P.F.C., Kerry, R., Lee, D, & Turner, S.W. (1995). *An open trial of exposure therapy based on deconditioning for posttraumatic stress disorder.* British Journal of Clinical Psychology. 31, 407-416.

Trickett, D. & Putnam, F. (1993). *Impact of child sexual abuse in females: toward a developmental psychobiological integration.* Psychological Science. 4, 81-87.

Udwin, O. (1993). *Annotation: Children's reactions to traumatic events.* Journal of Child Psychology & Psychiatry & Allied Disciplines. 34, 115-127.

van der Kolk (1994). *The body keeps the score: Memory and the evolving psychobiology of PTSD.* Harvard Review of Psychiatry. 1, 253 -265.

van der Kolk, B.A. (1987). Psychological Trauma. Washington, D.C. American Psychiatric Press

van der Kolk, B., Roth, S., Pelcovitz, D. & Mandel, F. (1993). *Complex post traumatic stress disorder: Results from the DSM-IV field trial of PTSD.* In D. Meichenbaum. A Clinical Handbook/Practical Therapist Manual: For Assessing and Treating Adults with Post-Traumatic Stress Disorder (PTSD), Waterloo, Ontario, Canada Institute Press.

van der Kolk, B., McFarlane, A., & Weisaeth, L. (1996). (Eds.). Traumatic Stress Disorder: The Effects of Overwhelming Experience on Mind, Body, and Society. New York, The Guilford Press.

Vernberg, E., Eric, M., LaGreca, A., Silverman, W. & Prinstein, M. (1996). *Prediction of posttraumatic stress symptoms in children after hurricane andrew.* Journal of Abnormal Psychology. 105, 237-248.

Vogel, J. & Vernberg, E. (1993). *Children's psychological responses to disaster.* Journal of Child Psychology. 22, 470-484.

Wallen, J. (1993). *Protecting the mental health of children in dangerous neighborhoods.* Children Today. 22, 24-27.

Webb, N. (Ed.) (1991). Play Therapy with Children In Crisis. New York: Guilford.

World Health Organization (1992). The ICD-10 Classification of Mental and Behavioral Disorders: Clinical Descriptions and Guidelines. Geneva

Yule, W. & Udwin, O. (1991). *Screening child aurvivors for post-traumatic stress disorders: Experiences from the "Jupiter" sinking.* British Journal of Clinical Psychology. 30, 131-138.

Yule, W. (1992). *Post-traumatic stress disorder in child survivors of shipping disasters: The sinking of the "Jupiter".* Psychotherapy and Psychosomatics 57, 200-205.

AUTHORS INDEX

Abberant, J., 35
Ackerman, P., 1
Anderson, B., 23
Arroya, E., 12, 13, 15
Baettig, D., 33
Beck, A., 32
Belenky, G., 21
Berent, S., 26
Beyers, S., 34
Black, D., 1
Bloch, D., 10
Bradburn, I., 14
Bradner, T., 10
Bremmer, J., 26
Cadwell, J., 23
Charlton, P., 24
Clum, G., 23
Cohen, S., 1, 12
Cooper, N., 23
Costanzo, P., 1, 44
Dancu, E., 24
Deblinger, E., 30, 76
Dykman, R., 1
Emery, P., 30
Eric, M., 1, 12
Ericksen, J., 5
Eth, S., 34, 37, 45, 161
Fairbank, J,. 23
Famularo, R., 12
Fenton, T., 12
Foa, E., 22, 24
Frankl, E., 24, 33
Frank, V., 10
Frederick, C., 4
Freud, S., 5, 21, 29
Garbarino, J., 12
Gebarski, S., 26

Goetz, R., 10, 21
Grill, D., 25
Hembre, E., 24
Hendricks, J., 1
Herl, T., 13, 16
Herman, J., 13, 16
Irwin, C., 1,12
Jackson, L., 1, 12, 44
Johnson, D., 35
Johnson, K., 9, 152, 153, 161, 162
Kaplan, T., 1
Keane, T., 23
Kerry, R., 24
Kinscherff, R., 12
Klingman, A., 14
Koplewicz, H., 14
Kowalski, J., 15, 94, 159
Kozak, M., 22
LaGreca, A., 1, 12
Lang, P., 25
LeDoux, I., 26
Lippman, J., 30, 76
Lonnigan, C., 1
Malchiodi, C., 34
Malleson, N., 30
March, J., 1, 12, 44
Marks, I., 31
Matsakis, A., 13, 131
McFarlane, A., 1, 12, 15
Meichenbaum, D., 24, 33, 152, 158, 162, 182
Mihaescu, G., 33
Milgram, N., 14
Mower, O., 31
Nader, K., 1, 12, 13, 15, 40, 51, 75
Pelcovicz, D., 13
Perry, B., 26

Peterson, S., 9
Piers, C., 20, 22, 29, 30
Pynoos, R., 8, 12, 13, 15, 34, 37, 45, 75, 158, 161
Quarentelli, E. 10
Rachman, S., 31
Raider, M., 2, 12, 154
Riley, S., 34
Roje, J., 35
Romanski, L., 26
Roth, S., 13
Rothschild, B., 2
Saigh, P., 12, 14, 15, 19, 23, 26, 31, 32, 157, 159
Santiago, A., 2, 79
Schwarzwald, J., 14
Shalev, A., 22, 157
Shaw, J., 14
Silverman, W., 1, 12
Stampfl, T., 7, 31
Starknum, M., 26
Steele, W., 2, 79, 154, 183
Steer, R., 30, 76
Stewart, B., 33
Straub, R., 9
Stubner, M., 12
Terr, L., 9, 13, 16, 67
Thompson, J., 14
Toubiana, D., 12
Trickett, D., 12
Udwin, O., 9
Ursano, R., 22
van der Kolk, B., 2, 5, 11, 13, 15, 17, 19, 20, 21, 25, 26, 29, 31, 75, 94
Vernberg, E., 1, 12, 75
Vogel, J., 75
Waysman, M., 14

Webb, N., 35
Weisenber, M., 14
Wallen, J., 12
Yasuda, P., 1, 12
Yule, W., 1, 9, 12, 157

INDEX

Abreact, 20, 22
Abuse, 30, 39-41
  age as a variable, 60
  all forms, 39-41
  type of, 67
  intervention, 76, 202, 205, 206
  threats to abuse, 135
  trauma severity, 154
Accidents, 1, 14
Accountability, 27, 72, 86, 98-100
Adolescents,
  adolescent symptomatology, 8
  future orientation, 101-103
  response to drawing, 198
Age,
  as a variable, 60
  reactions at age levels, 8
  age boundaries, 67-68
  preschool, 9, 81, 86, 89, 161, 162
Aggression, 9, 26, 13
APA, 5, 6, 10, 11, 13, 51, 101
Analysis,
  quantitative, 39-41
  research analysis, 54-59
  multivariate analysis, 60-61
Anger, (see violence) 135, 136, 155
  rage, 135, 136
Anxiety, 9, 22, 31, 32
  anxiety management, 25-26, 33
  parental anxiety, 108-111
Arousal, 10, 19, 51, 52, 54, 58, 59, 60,
  hyperarousal, 2, 26, 68
  symptoms of, 7-8
  state of, 25-27
Assessment, 8, 38, 44, 46, 50, 53, 69, 87,
  107, 116-118, 182
Attachment, 8, 9, 29

ADHD, 26
Auditory, 29
Avoidance, 7, 29, 31, 35, 51-54, 116, 164,
  189

Biobehavioral, 29
Biological, 21, 205
Blame, 127
  see accountability

Cardiac Neurosis 5, 19
Central nervous system, 26
Child Adolescent Questionnaire, 58, 84, 96
Child Reaction Index, 37
Classical conditioning, 31
Classroom presentation, 79, 160, 168, 180
  (see debriefing)
Concentration, 8, 9, 10, 81
Confidentiality, 46, 167, 169, 191
Cognitive, 2, 8, 9, 20, 23, 67, 71, 76, 94,
  100, 103, 105, 115, 142, 153, 161, 175,
  192
  behavioral, 174
  reframing, 35, 45, 46, 49, 50, 63, 68, 74,
  78, 101, 107, 122, 130-138, 144, 177,
  188, 199
  reorder(ing), 23, 74, 98, 116, 140, 189
  therapy, 24, 25, 32, 33
Combat, 13, 15, 19, 20, 21, 23
Comorbidity, 194
  premorbid, 10
Consciousness, 8, 20, 22, 30, 31, 34, 35
Crisis, 108
  intervention, 3, 151, 152
  reframing, 139

Debriefing, 151-186
　classroom presentation, 79, 160, 168, 180
　crisis team debriefing, 79
　critical incident stress, 151, 153, 167
　group stress debriefing, 22
　operational debriefing, 79, 151, 163, 177, 188
　parents, 112, 113-114
　questions about, 158-173
Denial, 16, 79, 127, 151, 161, 187, 188
Desensitization, 22, 23, 26
Detachment, 7, 8, 101, 111
Disaster, 75, 154,158, 160, 164, 167, 182
Disbelief, 79, 127
Disorders,
　Acute Stress Disorders, 3, 11, 53, 154, 155,156, 159, 161, 182, 185, 187, 188, 192
　　Gross Stress Reaction, 5, 10
　　of extreme stress, 75
　　Posttraumatic Stress Disorder (PTSD), 1, 3, 5, 6, 9-13, 19, 22, 38, 100, 108, 136, 153-156, 182
　　diagnostic criteria, 6-8
Dissociation, 26, 33
Divorce, 1, 6, 12, 39, 40, 43, 53, 67, 104, 110, 154
Drawing, 33-35, 71, 72, 195-198
Dreams, 7, 111, 117, 155
DSM-IV, 6, 11, 13, 14, 51, 52, 70, 76, 95, 101, 136, 187
Dysfunctional, 24, 25, 32, 33

Education, 42, 50, 57, 66, 69, 75, 79, 84, 86, 100, 110, 118, 158, 173, 175
Ethnicity, 57, 60, 67, 119

Exposure,
　exposure based treatment, 30-31
　techniques, 31-32, 118
　"imaginal", 23, 24
　"in vivo", 23, 24, 34
　most exposed, 80, 151, 152, 160, 163, 174-176, 187, 188
　types of, 159-160
　victim exposure, 13-15
Externalization, 34, 71, 177
EMDR, 26

Family, 11, 15, 39, 44, 53, 68, 94, 95, 109-117, 125, 127, 143-149, 153, 159, 160, 166, 176, 188, 206,
Fear, 45, 48, 111, 112, 118, 123, 125
　diagnostic criteria, 6, 8
　reduction of, 23, 24
　fear response, 31, 32
　sensation of, 64, 65
　reframing of, 74
Female (see gender), 15, 24, 94
Fight, 25, 100
Fire, 15, 38, 39, 40, 159
Flashback, 7, 111
Flight, 25, 100
Flooding, 34, 162
Foreshortened Future, 7, 111
Future orientation, 86, 101
Foster care, 45, 53, 191

Goals (of SITCAP), 70
Grief, 1, 8, 39, 44, 52, 66-69, 76, 78, 84, 109, 110, 155, 158, 171, 185
Guilt, 8, 19, 13, 72, 127, 155
　(see accountability)
Gender, 5, 7, 60, 67, 119

Healing Benchmarks, 118, 134, 140, 142, 143
Helplessness, 6, 13, 100
Hopelessness, 86, 100, 129, 132
Hormones, 25
  neurohormonal, 25
Horror, 6, 171
Hurricane, 14
Hurt, 27, 45,
  questions about, 66, 72
  reframing, 133
  session about, 86, 97-98
Hyperactivity, 192
Hypervigilance, 89, 112, 155
Hypnosis, 21, 158
Hysteria, 5, 20, 161

Incident type, 15
  nature of, 16, 17
Industrial trauma, 21
Interventions, 19-21, 26
  adult, 19-25
  children, 29-35
  field-testing of, 37-45
  evaluation of, 45-48, 49-61
  overview (SITCAP), 63-81
  parent, 107-150
  school, 151-152 (see debriefing)
  strategies of, 83-105
Intrusive, 7, 9, 29, 72, 84, 111, 166
Images, 2, 7, 9, 25-29, 35, 64, 111, 166, 172
Immune system, 25, 192
Implosive, 31
Irritability, 8, 9, 19, 21, 112, 136

Limbic areas, 26
Language, 32, 34, 51, 71, 87, 98

Magical thinking, 68
Medication, 25, 57, 59, 114, 135, 136, 139, 143
Medical procedures, 1, 12
Murder, 38-43, 53, 65, 77, 97, 154, 159, 202
Memory,
  body, 1
  contextual, 33
  declarative, 26
  false memory, 202
  fixed, 29
  impairment, 9
  implicit, 2, 26
  recall, 7, 23, 111,119, 120, 133, 168, 193
  repressed, 34
  retain (retention), 162 192, 193
  short term, 26, 68
  traumatic memory, 23, 25, 26, 31-34, 123, 148, 149
Male (see gender), 15, 57, 93
Mind-body origins, 19

Narcosynthesis, 21
Natural disasters, 1, 12, 35, 44, 67
Neocortex, 26
Neurocirculatory asteria, 19
Neuronal excitability, 26
Nightmares, 9, 10, 206
Normal, 5, 7, 10, 11, 22, 25, 67, 111, 116, 119, 140, 152, 157, 187
Normalize, 50, 88, 91, 100, 115, 118, 134, 172-174, 178, 180, 190, 199

Organic, 5, 19, 20

Parent, 38-42, 52-55, 59, 200
  interventions 107-150
Parent involvement, 75-79, 83-87
Parent Questionnaire, 51-55, 59
Pathological Traumatic Syndrome, 21
Personal involvement, 14
Physical proximity, 13, 44, 68
Physiology, 7, 19, 25, 26, 111
Powerlessness, 27, 70, 86, 98, 100, 118,
  129, 135, 138, 167, 182, 195
Psychological, 2, 5, 7, 19, 20, 111, 200
Psychomotor, 50, 71, 120, 130, 148, 177,
  199
Psychophysiological, 25
Rape, 11, 15, 23, 24, 33, 35, 38
Recapitulation, 118, 124
Reexperiencing, 23, 29, 31, 35, 84, 116
Regression, 60
Repetitive play, 7, 9
Research,
  history of, 1-17, 19-27
  intervention, 30-35
  SITCAP (research), 37-62
Resource Materials, 44, 66, 69, 108
Revenge, 27, 42, 45, 50, 64, 69, 70, 74, 80,
  86, 98-100, 118, 123, 134

Safety, 27, 43, 45, 63, 65, 74, 77, 87, 155,
  183-185, 199, 200
  safe place, 115, 122, 131, 133, 147, 191,
  194
Secondary Victimization, 118, 126, 127,
  129, 182
  wounding, 79, 127

Sensory, 2, 30, 35, 89, 92, 94-98, 101-105
  nature of, 26
Sensations, 25, 68-70, 114, 118, 148, 190,
  191
  of trauma, 2, 64, 67, 85, 86
  sensorimotor, 33
  sensory oriented, 22
  sensory relief, 27, 121-122, 133-34
Shame, 8, 9, 73-74, 100, 189
Shell Shock, 5, 20
Siblings, 189
Sleep, 8, 9, 111, 117, 143, 197
Soldiers, 5, 10, 19, 20, 145
Somatic, 8, 21, 182
Stress, 10, 11, 19, 25, 44, 154, 157, 170,
  182, 185, 193
  (see acute disorder)
  (see extreme disorder)
  PTSD (see disorder)
Stress Inoculation, 22, 24, 33
Story
  Brave Bart 89-91
  telling the, 63, 65, 68, 71, 92
  (see Trauma Narrative)
Substance Abuse, 38-41, 44, 135
Suicide, 38-41, 53, 67, 98, 100, 101, 110,
  132, 135, 154, 159, 160, 181,182, 204
Survivor, 27, 51, 69, 77, 80, 90, 101
  as a survivor, 123-126, 130-131
  becoming a survivor, 132-135
  survivor guilt, 9, 13, 72, 100,
  survivor plan, 132, 143-145
  survivor thinking, 24, 33, 45, 64, 74, 81,
  86, 87, 94, 102, 118, 125, 144, 194
  survivor response, 94, 127, 134, 136, 173

Thought Field Therapy, 26
Transient situational disturbance, 5, 10
Trauma Institute (TLC), 27, 35, 37, 38, 137, 153, 158, 163, 202-207
Trauma narrative, 23, 31-35, 46, 49, 50, 63, 80, 147
  examples of, 72-74, 92-103
Trauma reactions, 6, 10, 12, 16, 17, 20, 24, 31, 66, 84-89, 109, 112, 122, 125, 133, 140, 141, 155-159, 172, 178
  severity levels, 15, 85, 95, 96, 116, 137, 140
Trauma questions, 42, 52, 69, 72, 73, 80, 88, 118, 141
Trauma Response Kit, 49, 53, 60
Trauma syndrome, 11
Trauma themes, 72, 77, 124
Trauma training, 24, 52, 53, 74, 76, 80, 103, 105, 109, 120, 146, 166, 185, 204, 207
Trauma triggers, 25, 26, 29, 71, 78, 100, 155, 188, 194
Trauma type, 13, 16, 17, 67

Variable, 95, 137
  independent, 41, 49
  dependent, 16, 51
Vicarious traumatization, 159, 166, 180
Victimization, 14, 42, 99, 118, 120, 132, 135, 182
  secondary wounding, 79, 127, 129
Victim response, 129, 173
Victim thinking, 24, 33, 45, 74, 80, 87, 125, 126, 129, 132, 144

Violence,
  assaultive, 1, 7, 48, 60, 67, 97, 98, 155
  non-assaultive (violent) 2, 3, 7, 41, 43, 48, 60, 68, 155, 159, 165
Visual, 29, 35, 44, 64, 71, 77, 94, 103, 118, 150,
Visual Kinesthetic Dissociation (VKD), 26
Vulnerability, 8, 9, 12-16, 61, 84, 136, 154, 182, 188

Witness,
  exposure to, 159
  making us a witness to, 113, 118, 145, 149, 177, 191
Worksheets, 48, 81, 93, 102, 104, 130, 141, 143
Worry, 15, 16, 27, 45-48, 64, 69, 70, 72, 80, 86
  examples of, 94-97, 123, 137-140
Worst part, 73, 74, 100, 104, 115, 121, 191

MELLEN STUDIES IN SOCIAL WORK

1. William Steele and Melvyn Raider, **Structured Sensory Intervention for Traumatized Children, Adolescents and Parents: Strategies to Alleviate Trauma**
2. Luisa Stormer Deprez, **The Family Support Act of 1988: A Case Study of Welfare Policy in the 1980s**
3. Andrew W. Dobelstein, **The 1996 Federal Welfare Reform in North Carolina: The Politics of Bureaucratic Behavior**
4. Janice Gasker, **Incorporating Sexual Trauma into the Functional Life Narrative**
5. Anne L. Cummings and Alan W. Leschied (eds.), **Research and Treatment for Aggression with Adolescent Girls**
6. Steven R. Smith, **Defending Justice as Reciprocity–An Essay on Social Policy and Political Philosophy**